Leo Marriott

Britannia
Prestwick-Orlando

Howdy! Hola! Bonjour! Guten Tag!

bookcrossing.com

I'm a *very special book*, you see, I'm travelling around the world making new friends. I hope I've met another friend in you. Please go to

www.BookCrossing.com

and enter my BCID number (shown below). You'll discover where I've been and who has read me, and I can let them know I'm safe here in your hands.

Then... *READ and RELEASE me!*

BCID: 620 — 8561817

On stand. India Golf is safely parked at Gate 24 Orlando International.

LONDON

IAN ALLAN LTD

First published 1991

ISBN 0 7110 1996 7

Published by Ian Allan Ltd, Shepperton,
Surrey; and printed by Ian Allan Printing Ltd
at their works at Coombelands in
Runnymede, England

Front cover:
**A Britannia 767 waits for permission
to proceed prior to take-off.**

Back cover, top:
A quiet moment on the flightdeck.

Back cover, bottom:
**Airside Two, one of three
satellite terminals at Orlando.**

Contents

Acknowledgements

A book such as this can only be written and produced with the complete co-operation of the airline concerned. In this case Britannia Airways gave their wholehearted and enthusiastic support to the project from its inception right through to publication and I am pleased to be able to record the names of some of those concerned.

The airline's Public Relations department is run by the energetic Richard Hedges who, with his assistants, provided the necessary initial contact and supplied photographs and background material in abundance. In order to gather information on the operation of the Boeing 767, I made several flights in addition to the one described in this book and the pilot's involved on those occasions were Capt Steve Coles and 1st Off Stuart Goldspink, and Capt Graham Anderson and 1st Off Simon Storah. Britannia's Chief Pilot, Capt C. F. M. Norman and the B767 Fleet Captain, Capt Paul Watson, both gave their blessing and active encouragement to the writing of the book.

Of course, special mention must be made of Capt Graham Freeman and 1st Off Ben Johnson who crewed the flight which is the main subject of this book. They, as with the other crews, calmly put up with my intrusion of their flight-deck complete with cameras, notebooks and tape recorders. Nine-and-a-half hours is a long time for complete strangers to be thrown together and I always approach such assignments with some trepidation. I can only say that I was made to feel completely welcome and at home throughout the flight and, indeed, during my subsequent stay on the ground at Orlando. I hope that they will feel that this book goes some way towards explaining to a wide range of readers — including many of their future passengers — the complex job that they do.

Mention must also be made of the cabin crews, particularly Gloria Barrett and her happy band on the return BAL137B from Orlando to Manchester. Although the job of the pilots is well documented, the cabin crews on long haul flights must work continuously for up to 10hrs at a time while maintaining the high standard of service to 274 passengers aboard each Boeing 767. Thanks to you all.

Finally, mention should be made of people outside the airline who also contributed including Cheryl Arnts at Orlando Airport, and the public relations officers at Prestwick and the Civil Aviation Authority, London, for the provision of various photographs.

The aeronautical charts reproduced in this book are virtually all produced by Aerad, a subsidiary of British Airways, which has provided a complete selection of charts and plates covering the entire route of the aircraft. Sam Hall, the division's manager, was most co-operative and his help is much appreciated.

Left:
The wide-bodied Boeing 767 is the pride of Britannia's modern jet fleet. *Britannia*

Glossary and Abbreviations

AFCS   Automatic Flight Control System — the autopilot
AIDS   Airborne Integrated Data System
APU   Auxiliary Power Unit
ARCC   Air Route Control Centre (American equivalent of the British ATCC — Air Traffic Control Centre)
ASI   Airspeed Indicator
ATC   Air Traffic Control
ATIS   Automatic Terminal Information System
BAL   ICAO (*qv*) Code for Britannia Airways for ATC purposes
C   Centigrade or Celsius
CAA   Civil Aviation Authority (British)
CDU   Control and Display Unit, part of the FMS (*qv*)
CF   Critical Fuel
CP   Critical Point
C of G   Centre of Gravity
cps   cycles per second
DME   Distance Measuring Equipment — usually associated with a VOR (*qv*) and enables the pilot to read off his distance from the DME station
EADI   Electronic Attitude and Director Indicator
EFIS   Electronic Flight Information System
EGT   Exhaust Gas Temperature
EHSI   Electronic Horizontal Situation Indicator
EICAS   Engine Indicating and Crew Alerting System
ER   Extended Range
EROPS   Extended Range Operations
ETOPS   Extended Range Twinjet Operations
FAA   Federal Aviation Authority (US)
FL   Flight Level (aircraft altitude assuming standard sea level air pressure of 1,013mb)
FMS   Flight Management System
HF   High Frequency (radio)
HP   High Pressure
hz   Hertz (1cps)
IAS   Indicated Airspeed
ICAO   International Civil Aviation Organisation
ILS   Instrument Landing System
INS   Inertial Navigation System
IRS   Inertial Reference System (generally accepted as referring to an INS which incorporates laser gyro platforms)
kgs   Kilogrammes

L   Left
LNAV   Lateral Navigation — autopilot mode
M   Magnetic
mb   Millibars
MHz   Mega Hertz (1,000cps)
MNPS   Minimum Navigation Performance Specification
N   North
N1   Engine fan speed expressed as a percentage of the nominal maximum rpm
N2   Engine first stage turbine speed expressed as a percentage of the nominal maximum rpm
NAT   North Atlantic
NDB   Non Directional Radio Beacon. A medium frequency navigation aid which provides a bearing but no track guidance
nm   Nautical Miles
OACC   Oceanic Area Control Centre
OCA   Oceanic Control Area
Okta   An eighth. Used in weather reports when describing amounts of sky obscured by cloud layers
QNH   Radio code group referring to the atmospheric pressure at sea level at a particular location. This value needs to be set on an altimeter's subscale so that it will read correctly
R   Right
RCAF   Royal Canadian Air Force
RTO   Rejected Take-Off
R/W   Runway
ScATCC   Scottish Air Traffic Control Centre
TAS   True Airspeed (Indicated Airspeed corrected for altitude and temperature)
TC   Top of Climb
TD   Top of Descent
TMA   Terminal Manoeuvring Area
tonne   Metric ton (1,000kg or 2,200lb)
UTC   Universal Co-ordinated Time
VFR   Visual Flight Rules
VHF   Very High Frequency (radio)
VNAV   Vertical Navigation — autopilot mode
VOR   VHF Omni Directional Radio Range — radio navigation aid whereby the pilot can determine his lateral displacement from a preset bearing or radial
VSI   Vertical Speed Indicator
W   West
WPT   Waypoint

Introduction

'The British are coming!' Just over 200 years ago, during the American War of Independence, this cry would have roused the good citizens of the State of Florida to reach for their guns and fight the redcoated soldiers of their colonial masters. Today the British are still coming to the 'Sunshine State' in their thousands, but this time as tourists and holidaymakers ready to marvel at and enjoy the achievements of the American way of life.

Since World War 2, when American GIs poured into Britain bringing a taste of their culture and lifestyle, and the products of Hollywood filled our cinema screens, the United States has continued to hold a fascination for the British. For many years the cost of travel, either by air or sea, prevented all but a few from making the journey. The introduction of transatlantic jet airliners began to change this picture, particularly when the first wide-bodied aircraft such as the Boeing 747 and DC-10 entered service in the early 1970s. Even so, the idea of a family holiday across the Atlantic was still something only to be contemplated by those with plenty of money to spare. Now this has all changed and the cost of a holiday in America, and other far flung parts of the world, costs little more than a fortnight's stay at one of the traditional (and overcrowded) Mediterranean resorts.

What has brought about this revolution? The answer, in a nutshell, is technology in the form

Above:

Britannia Airways has a long association with the Boeing Company which goes back to 1968 when the airline became the first European operator of the now best-selling Boeing 737-200. In 1984 they were again the first European airline with the wide-bodied Boeing 767 and it was entirely fitting that Boeing's 6,000th jet airliner should be handed over to Britannia in April 1990. *Britannia*

of advanced modern airliners equipped with the latest electronic navigation and control systems and powered by only two ultra reliable fuel-efficient engines. The vital factor is the use of twin-engined aircraft, with obvious economies of operation, on long overwater routes which hitherto have required multi-engined aircraft to maintain an acceptable safety factor in the event of a single engine failure at any stage of the flight.

By the early 1980s the new generation of big fanned turbojet engines such as Rolls-Royce's RB211 and General Electric's CF6 had shown thousands of hours reliable operation aboard the Boeing 747 and other aircraft. Airline operators, backed by airframe and engine manufacturers, began to question the need for unduly restrictive regulations framed when engine technology was less mature. In particular the International Civil Aviation Organisation (ICAO) and various national regulatory bodies laid down that any

twin-engined aircraft should not be flown such that it was more than 60min flying time at single engine cruise speed from a suitable diversion airfield. Although it was theoretically possible to fly the Atlantic under this rule, the necessary route was anything but direct and the fickle weather at some of the diversion airfields in Arctic regions made such flights impossible from a commercial viewpoint.

As in many fields of aviation, the driving force for change came from American airlines with their need to serve destinations such as Hawaii and various Caribbean points. Thus grew up the concept of Extended Range Twin Engine Operations (ETOPS), now restyled Extended Range Operations (EROPS). Although this will be examined in more detail later in the book, at this stage it is sufficient to realise that for an airline to gain approval for EROPS, it must be equipped with aircraft powered by engines which have already demonstrated a specified degree of in-service reliability, it must show that its maintenance methods and schedules meet exceptionally high standards, and the pilots must be familiar with the appropriate methods of operation which must be laid down in the airline's operations manual. In addition, the aircraft must be suitably modified and equipped to EROPS standards.

British airlines, particularly those involved in the Inclusive Tour (IT) market, were quick to see the commercial possibilities offered by EROPS. Operators such as Air 2000, Air Europe and Monarch began transatlantic flying in 1988 using the twin-engine Boeing 757 which could seat around 204 passengers in tourist configuration. In the meantime Britannia Airways, Britain's biggest charter airline, gained EROPS approval for its fleet of Boeing 767-200ER aircraft and in November 1988 began a series of charters to Australia routeing through Bahrain and Singapore. The following year, direct flights from UK airports were launched to a variety of exotic destinations including Montego Bay, Barbados and Orlando. Currently this programme has been expanded to include other destinations including Canada and New Zealand. It is all a far cry from Britannia's first package holiday flights to Spain in 1962 using piston-engined Constellations.

Today's flights represent a return to transatlantic flying for Britannia after a gap of 16 years. Earlier attempts at tapping this market using two Boeing 707-320 aircraft were halted by the rocketing price of fuel in the early 1970s. However by 1990 the airline had over a dozen flights a week crossing the Atlantic, each carrying up to 274 passengers in twin-aisle comfort with a full range of inflight service including meals, drinks and films. This book traces the course of one of these flights — from Prestwick in Scotland to Orlando, Florida.

Prestwick, of course, has a long association with transatlantic flying and in the days of piston-engined airliners was the main British terminal for eastbound flights. Today its future is uncertain because recent government policy decisions have removed its gateway status to allow transatlantic flights serving Scotland to operate from nearby Glasgow. Orlando, at the end of the route, offers a completely different scenario and is one of America's fastest growing airports with almost 17 million passengers passing through its modern terminal in 1989. Florida, known as the 'Sunshine State', is home to a wealth of world famous attractions including Epcot, Disney World and the Kennedy Space Center as well as being blessed with hundreds of miles of white sun soaked beaches. It is little wonder that it is now one of the top destinations for the British holidaymaker.

Our flight will be in a Boeing 767-200ER — one of the world's most sophisticated commercial aircraft. First flown in 1981, the aircraft entered service the following year with United Airlines. Britannia Airways was the first European operator of the type, receiving its first aircraft in 1984 and currently operates eight -200 and -200ER variants. Although conventional in appearance, the Boeing 767 is an extremely advanced aircraft making great use of modern digital avionics for flight control, navigation and instrumentation. The best way to understand and appreciate the workings of this big aircraft is – From the Flightdeck!

Above left:
The Kennedy Space Center is one of several major tourist attractions situated in the 'Sunshine State' of Florida.

Left:
Britannia's Boeing 767-200ER aircraft are powered by two General Electric CF6-80A turbofans which each develop 48,000lb. The massive first stage fan is over 7ft in diameter.

> **Publisher's note:**
> Since this book was written, Britannia has transferred its transatlantic services to Glasgow International.

The Flightdeck

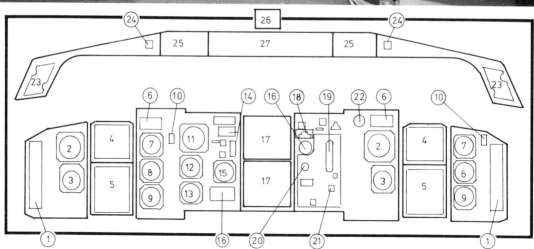

A general view of the 767's flightdeck. The use of modern electronic displays significantly reduces the amount of instrumentation compared with earlier generation aircraft. *Boeing*

The layout of the 767's flightdeck reflects Boeing's vast store of experience in building literally thousands of jet airliners. In fact the equipment and layout is identical to that of the sister design, the narrow-bodied 757, allowing airlines to obtain a common type rating on the two aircraft for their pilots. Both aircraft are significant in that they represent Boeing's entry into the use of electronic flight information systems instead of the conventional arrays of analogue flight instruments, giving rise to the so-called 'glass cockpit'. Boeing was not alone in introducing the new technology and faced fierce competition from the Europe-based Airbus Industrie. The 767 prototype first flew in 1981 but was closely followed by the rival A310 and A300-600, the latter being very close to the 767 in technical specification and performance. The resulting sales battles were extremely fierce and each and every order was hard won.

The layout of the 767 flightdeck is conventional with the two pilots seated either side of a central console and the instrument panel containing the six EFIS displays set in front of them. One of the launch customers for the 767 was United Airlines whose pilots originally insisted on a three-man crew. Consequently provision was made for a third pilot or a flight engineer sitting between and behind the others, and his seat was designed to slide and swivel so that he could face a systems control panel on the starboard side. By the time the aircraft was in production the demand for three-crew operation had almost gone and all aircraft system controls were integrated into the centre console or overhead panel where they could be easily reached by either pilot. Nevertheless the third pilot's seat remains and is useful when carrying out training flights or when supernumerary crew are aboard. The Australian airline QANTAS was

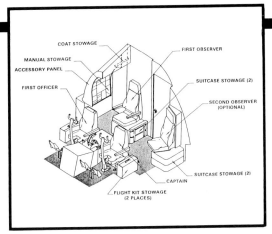

Above:
Boeing 767 Flightdeck Arrangement. *Boeing*

the only one to retain a third pilot when its aircraft entered service in 1985. In addition there is a fourth seat tucked into the after port side of the flightdeck. The flightdeck is roomy and there is plenty of carefully thought out stowage for items such as charts, technical logs and aircraft operating manuals, all positioned where they can be reached in flight. In the rear righthand corner is a small wardrobe area for hanging uniforms and stowing caps.

The six EFIS and EICAS colour displays are manufactured by Rockwell Collins. In front of each pilot is an electronic attitude director indicator (EADI) with an electronic horizontal situation indicator (EHSI) mounted below. Each of these displays is fed by one of three symbol generators, one each for the captain and first officer, and a back-up unit for redundancy. In emergency conditions, all vital information can be displayed from one symbol generator which automatically switches to a special reversionary mode. Automatic circuits quickly adapt the dis-

Main Instrument Panel — key to drawing	
1 Instrument Switching	14 Caution/Warning Displays
2 Airspeed Indicator (ASI)	15 Standby Engine Display
3 Radio Magnetic Indicator (RMI)	16 Flap Position
4 Electronic Attitude Director Indicator (EADI)	17 Engine Indicator and Crew Alerting System (EICAS)
5 Electronic Horizontal Situation Indicator (EHSI)	18 Engine Mode Selector
6 Autoland Indicator	19 Landing Gear Selector
7 Altimeter	20 Alternate Flap
8 Vertical Speed Indicator (VSI)	21 Alternate Landing Gear
9 Clock	22 Brake Pressure
10 ILS Marker Beacon	23 Lighting Control Panel
11 Standby Artificial Horizon	24 Master Caution and Warning
12 Standby Airspeed Indicator	25 VOR/Course Selectors
13 Standby Altimeter	26 Standby Compass
	27 Auto Pilot — Auto Throttle — Flight Director Selectors

Above:
The Boeing 767 shares the same flightdeck as its sister design, the narrow-bodied Boeing 757. Britannia is currently operating both aircraft and its pilots hold a common type rating, allowing a considerable reduction in crew training and staffing costs. *Boeing*

Right:
The Electronic Altitude Director Indicator (EADI) is one of two primary flight displays available to each pilot. In the centre is the artificial horizon and pitch indicator while groundspeed and altitude are shown at top left and right respectively. The symbols on the left show if the aircraft is flying fast or slow in respect of a preset airspeed, while the righthand side shows deviation from a required glideslope or pitch angle. Captions along the lower edge of the display show which autopilot modes are in operation.

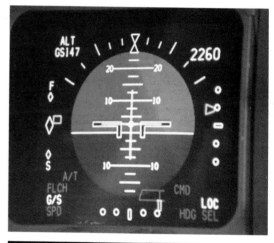

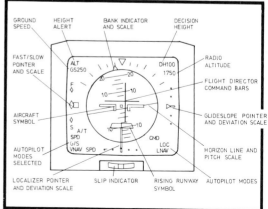

play brightness to cope with ambient light conditions which may range from total darkness at night to direct sunlight at high altitude. In considering the cost of such equipment it is sobering to reflect that the symbol generators alone cost around £50,000 per aircraft.

The EADI display includes ground speed, radio altitude, ILS localiser and glideslope deviation information on approach, as well as speed command and basic roll and pitch data. Each customer airline can specify the manner in which data is presented and Britannia's displays show the amount by which airspeed varies from a preset target. Actual speed is shown on a sep-

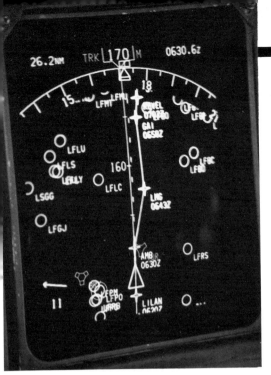

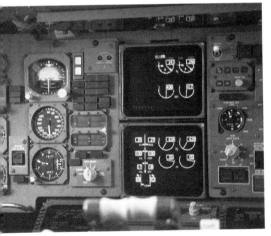

arate ASI. Autopilot and thrust management
mode indications are also shown on the EADI.

The EHSI can be selected to operate in one of
five modes including the traditional compass
rose, ILS or VOR modes, a map mode showing
the aircraft's position relative to various waypoints, and a north-orientated map mode showing the flight plan. Of these the MAP mode is
used almost exclusively except that the ILS
mode is normally selected when making an
approach. In addition the weather radar picture
can be superimposed in full colour to show the
disposition and severity of significant weather.
The radar will, of course, also show geographic
features such as rivers and coastlines if the
aerial is depressed to an appropriate angle.

In the centre of the instrument panel, visible
to both pilots, are the two Engine Indication and
Crew Alerting System (EICAS) displays. These
replace virtually all analogue instrumentation
which would have been used to show engine
performance parameters as well as the functioning of the various aircraft systems including
fuel, electrics and hydraulics. In fact there are
over 400 analogue, digital and discrete interfaces from the engines and subsystems to the
two EICAS computers which reproduce selected
data on the displays in both digital and analogue
format.

The centralised caution/warning system monitors over 200 functions and produces colour-
coded alerts and warnings which are automatically displayed on the lefthand side of the upper
display. On the ground, the lower display is
available for use by maintenance engineers who
can obtain data on engine and system performance during the previous flight. In addition,
various test functions are built in.

In-service experience with EFIS has shown
that the electronic components are achieving
unprecedented levels of reliability with serious
failures virtually unknown. In fact Collins
claims that some components are more than
seven times as reliable as the original
specification demanded. Despite this situation,

Autopilot mode selector panel

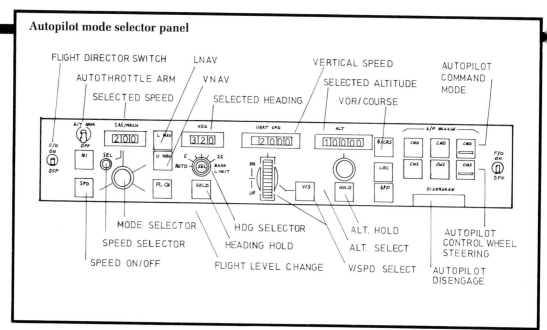

Right:

Part of the autopilot mode selector panel set into the glareshield above the main instrument panel. The three control knobs can be used to set required values for speed, heading and altitude, while the push buttons select various operating modes for the highly sophisticated Automatic Flight Control System.

both Boeing and the various airworthiness authorities have deemed it necessary to provide a full back-up of conventional instrumentation to cover the unlikely event of a total EFIS failure. Consequently the EFIS is backed up by analogue ASI, altimeter, VSI and artificial horizon, while engine parameters can be shown in digital form on a standby LED display.

Above the main instrument panel is a separate console mounted in the glareshield which carries the autopilot controls as well as ILS and VOR frequency selectors. A highly automated aircraft such as the 767 is almost entirely flown through the autopilot, as will be seen in the following pages. On the 767 the autopilot functions are coordinated by the Automatic Flight Control System (AFCS) which consists of triple Collins FCS-700A autopilot/flight directors and FCC-702 flight control computers. The latter unit processes information from various sources including air data units, the Inertial Reference System (IRS), and Flight Management System (FMS) computer so that the autopilot can perform tasks associated with flight director commands, speed, altitude and heading selection, and autolandings.

In flight, only one autopilot channel is normally selected but the other two continue to function in parallel providing instant back-up in the event of a failure. In addition, signals from all three channels are continually monitored and cross-checked to prove system integrity — this is particularly important when carrying out fully automatic landings.

Between the two pilots a central console carries the conventionally positioned throttle levers flanked by speedbrake, trim and flap controls (the undercarriage selector and indicators are mounted on the instrument panel in front of the First Officer). The rear of the console houses the VHF radio frequency selectors, pilots' communications systems, ADF frequency selectors, APU controls and engine fire suppression controls.

In front of the throttle quadrants are the two Control and Display Units (CDU) which allow each pilot to access the FMS computer. The FMS is the prime interface between the aircraft and the crew and is the key to the efficient and

Above:

The throttle quadrant is conventionally mounted between the two pilots. The levers on the left control trim and the speedbrakes, while the flap selector is to the right. The button set into the top of the thrust lever is a cutout for the autothrottle system.

Above right:

A centre panel behind the throttles houses selectors for the VHF radios, the ADF receiver and ATC transponder. In the centre is the Airborne Integrated Data System (AIDS) keyboard which can be used to access information stored in the air data computers.

Right:

Each pilot has a Control and Display Unit (CDU) which is used to programme the FMS computer with details of the flight. Subsequently the display will show information on the route and the progress of the flight including forecast ETAs and fuel states at each waypoint. The route data entered is also used by the FMS computer to generate the route map shown on the EHSI display.

economic operation of flight from take-off to landing. At the beginning of each flight the pilot enters details of the flight plan using the integral keyboard and the system then coordinates the functions of the navigation and autopilot systems in order to achieve the best flight profile while, at the same time, considerably reducing crew workload. When coupled to the AFCS, the FMS provides accurate engine thrust settings (through an autothrottle system) and flightpath guidance during all phases of flight, from immediately after take-off to final approach and land-

Above:

The overhead panel contains most of the controls for the aircraft's electrical, hydraulic, fuel and air conditioning systems.

ing. The system can predict the speeds and altitudes which will result in the best fuel economy and commands the aircraft to follow the most fuel efficient — or the 'least time' — flightpaths. The Honeywell Sperry FMS computer fitted to the 767 has a one-million word navigation database which holds details of all airports, navigation aids and routes within a specified area of operation (virtually worldwide in Britannia's case).

Although the 767 carries a full complement of radio navigation aids, the aircraft is able to continuously determine and update its position by means of a Honeywell Sperry HG1050 inertial reference system. As with the autopilot, there are three independent IRS platforms for fail-safe operation. Each platform uses state-of-the-art laser gyroscopes with no moving parts. Earlier inertial navigation systems based on mechanical gyros, despite being manufactured to the highest standards of precision, invariably suffer from cumulative position errors over a period of time.

In a laser gyro the laser beam is split and reflected in opposite directions around a triangular base platform. Any movement of the platform will result in a measurable phase difference of the two laser beams at their point of intersection, allowing accurate determination of the amount of movement. Provided that the IRS is correctly set up at the beginning of each flight, the system will have a virtually negligible position error, even after a flight lasting many hours and covering thousands of miles. In addition, warm up times are very short, around 3 or 4min, compared to almost 15min for earlier mechanical systems.

Although the IRS provides accurate position, attitude and heading data to the FMS, it also has a number of less obvious functions. For example, information on the aircraft's attitude is supplied to the fuel control computer which can use this data to correct readings from the fuel quantity sensors in each tank.

Controls for all auxiliary systems are located in the overhead panel set centrally into the flightdeck roof. On the lefthand side are the hydraulic and electrical system controls, IRS mode selectors, cockpit voice recorder, and a cluster of warning lights including indications of which cabin and hold doors are open. In the centre are the fuel system and anti-icing con-

trols, while the co-pilot's side includes controls for operating the air conditioning and heating in the passenger cabin and the cargo holds. Along the front edge of the overhead panel, easily reached by both pilots, are the various switches and rheostats for all aircraft lighting systems.

From the foregoing, the reader will have some appreciation of the degree of automation built into this aircraft. In fact there are no less than 140 microprocessors and computers aboard the 767 — a staggering figure. An incidental statistic is that there are 85 miles of wire in each aircraft, much of it accounted for by the necessity to pass data around the airframe from sensors to computers, and from computers to controls and systems.

Despite the degree of sophistication and automation, the designers have not excluded the pilot from the decision loop. Indeed, Boeing's philosophy has been to provide information and data in an easily assimilated form so that the pilots can continue to make the constant and necessary decisions required in the conduct of any flight quickly and safely. To this end the automation relieves the pilots of many routine and distracting tasks so that they can concentrate more easily on the overall safe operation of the flight. As this book will show, there is still plenty for them to do!

Preflight

A steady westerly breeze is blowing off the sea as Capt Graham Freeman and his First Officer, Ben Johnson arrive by taxi in front of Prestwick Airport's imposing terminal building just before midday on a summer Monday. In the clear visibility, so often prevailing along this part of the Scottish coast, the familiar landmarks of Ailsa Craig and the Isle of Arran can be easily seen across the white capped waves of the Firth of Clyde. However the two pilots have little time to contemplate the scenery as they enter the building and stride past the growing queues of expectant passengers waiting at the check-in desks. Today they are tasked with taking one of Britannia Airway's Boeing 767-200ER 150-tonne aircraft across the North Atlantic and down the east coast of the United States to Orlando in Florida — a 9-hr flight covering a distance of almost 4,000nm.

As a transatlantic terminal, Prestwick's heyday was during World War 2 when it was a major staging point for ferry flights, and in the following decade when the apron was often packed with Constellations, Stratocruisers and the various Douglas piston-engined airliners of the world's airlines. The airport's success hinged on its excellent fog-free weather record and the limited range capabilities of the immediate post-war generation of aircraft. The coming of the jets in the 1960s and 1970s with their greater range and sophisticated landing systems brought a drastic drop in the number of flights using Prestwick and today the commercial movements centre around a few weekly transatlantic charter flights to Canada and the United States.

One of these is the flight which will be described in this book — Britannia Airways Flight Number BAL316A. In common with all this airline's flights, the 'A' suffix denotes that it is outbound from the UK, while the return flight will bear the designation BAL316B indicating the return leg.

As this once-a-week flight is Britannia's only operation at Prestwick all ground support and handling, including passenger check-in, is contracted to Scottish Express (Scotex), a locally based handling agent. It is to their offices on the ground floor of the terminal, behind the rows of check-in desks, that Captain Freeman and his First Officer make their way. Here the pilots can carry out the necessary preflight planning and related paperwork before boarding the aircraft.

Left:
Captain Graham Freeman and First Officer Ben Johnson, the crew of Flight BAL316A to Orlando.

In fact, at this moment their aircraft (registration G-BRIG — Golf Bravo Romeo India Golf in phonetic parlance) is some 200 miles away, just taking off from East Midlands Airport with a number of passengers also bound for Orlando. This so-called split load technique is used by many operators to get the best payload for economic operation of long distance flights. This can lead to some complex aircraft and crew rostering as illustrated by India Golf's schedule for today. The aircraft started its day at Britannia's Luton base and carried out an empty ferry flight to East Midlands early in the morning, picking up 63 passengers before carrying on to Prestwick where it is due around 1230 local time. The pilots who have flown these two sectors will then return to Luton by road while Graham and Ben take over for the transatlantic sector, having travelled to Prestwick from Luton the previous day. As if this were not enough, the cabin crew of seven stewardesses are based at East Midlands and will accompany the flight right through to Orlando. These complex arrangements are necessary in order to ensure that all crew members do not work more than their legally laid down duty hours, although the allowable times vary according to the circumstances of the flight. In general, cabin staff are permitted to work slightly longer hours than flightdeck crews.

Although transatlantic flights have long since ceased to be a dramatic event, they still require careful and complex planning. In this day of computers and worldwide communications, Britannia's flight plans for transatlantic flights are provided by AMR Services, a subsidiary of American Airlines, based at Dallas/Fort Worth. Using the Lockheed Flight Planning Computer at Los Gatos, California, AMR produces a flight plan which will calculate the best route, generally the most fuel efficient, taking into account scheduled departure time, weather patterns, available alternate airfields, designated ATC routes across the Atlantic, estimated payload and a whole host of other details. The plan is produced following a request from Britannia's Operations Centre at Luton or by the handling agent at American airports for return flights.

The resulting flight plan is sent by teleprinter from Dallas to a convenient point for pick-up — normally to Britannia's or its agents' operations centre, but on occasions it could be sent directly to crews at their hotels. Running to several pages, the AMR plan tells the Captain everything he needs to know about the flight in great detail. As well as the actual route to be followed, it will also show the optimum level to fly at, the

Above:
The First Officer plots the day's North Atlantic Tracks on his chart.

Above right:
Captain Freeman discusses details of the flight with the Scotex Duty Operations Manager while waiting for the aircraft to arrive from East Midlands.

fuel which will be consumed on each leg, the exact latitude and longitude of the various way-points, the calculated take-off and landing weights of the aircraft, as well as meteorological information and relevant Notams. It also produces a flight log which pilots can use to record the actual progress of the flight and gives the exact format of the plan which should be filed with the ATC authorities before departure.

In the Scotex operations room at Prestwick Captain Freeman waits for a copy of the AMR plan for Flight BAL316A to come through by Fax from Britannia Ops at Luton. As this begins to come through, Ben Johnson takes a copy of the sheet giving the routeing and settles down to draw this on a North Atlantic plotting chart. Any pilot flying the North Atlantic will plot a route which will take most advantage of the pre-vailing wind and pressure system but with hun-dreds of flights a day making the crossing, severe congestion would occur on the optimum route. To prevent this potentially dangerous sit-

uation, the ATC authorities on both sides each day lay down a number of parallel tracks, nor-mally running 60nm apart, which are promul-gated from the Oceanic Control Centres at Prest-wick, Shannon and Gander to all airports and airlines. Pilots will then make up their flight plans utilising one of these laid down routes or tracks. Use of these routes is compulsory for air-craft flying through the Shanwick and Gander Oceanic Control Areas (OCAs) between Flight Levels 275 to 400 inclusively. The two OCAs form part of the larger North Atlantic Minimum Navigation Performance Specification (NAT MNPS) area in which aircraft are required to be equipped with onboard navigation systems capable of determining the aircraft's position to a high degree of accuracy. This is necessary in order to ensure that aircraft flying on the NAT track system maintain the requisite safe horizon-tal separation distances from other aircraft flying on parallel routes. The introduction of inertial navigation systems (INS) has made possible a greater utilisation of the airspace as the numbers of aircraft crossing the Atlantic has steadily increased.

First generation INS equipment using pre-cision gyro-based platforms allowed aircraft to follow routes 120nm apart but the latest systems use laser ring gyros with no moving parts to give unprecedented accuracy, and current horizontal separation is reduced to 60nm. Laser-based sys-tems are termed Inertial Reference Systems (IRS) to distinguish them from the earlier equip-

Chart showing the transatlantic sector of BAL.316A from Prestwick to the Canadian coast.

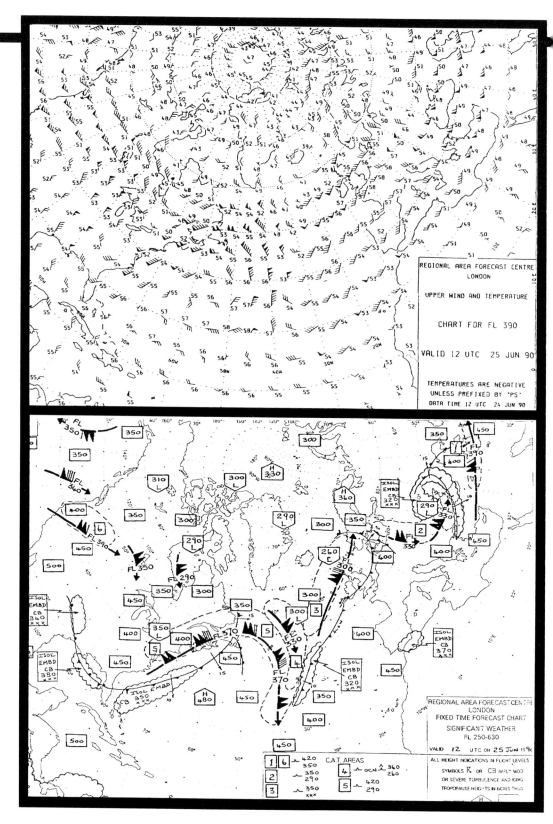

REGIONAL AREA FORECAST CENTRE
LONDON

UPPER WIND AND TEMPERATURE

CHART FOR FL 390

VALID 12 UTC   25 JUN 90

TEMPERATURES ARE NEGATIVE
UNLESS PREFIXED BY 'PS'
DATA TIME 12 UTC 24 JUN 90

REGIONAL AREA FORECAST CENTRE
LONDON
FIXED TIME FORECAST CHART
SIGNIFICANT WEATHER
FL 250-630

VALID 12 UTC ON 25 JUN 1990

ALL HEIGHT INDICATIONS IN FLIGHT LEVELS
SYMBOLS K OR CB IMPLY MOD
OR SEVERE TURBULENCE AND ICING
TROPOPAUSE HEIGHTS IN BOXES THUS

C.A.T. AREAS

ment. The Boeing 767 carries no less than three Honeywell Sperry IRS platforms which are integrated to an Attitude and Heading Reference System (AHRS) providing multi-axis data to the flight and navigation control and display systems of aircraft roll, pitch, heading and turn rate.

For today's flight to Orlando, the AMR flight plan has selected the northernmost of the promulgated routes (Track Alpha). This will take Flight BAL316A northwest from Prestwick to enter the Shanwick OCA at position 58.00 North 10.00 West. By convention this is abbreviated to 5810N and the route then passes through positions 6020N, 6030N, 6040N, 5850N to PORGY. The latter is one of the so called 'Fish' Points which mark the boundary between the Gander OCA and Canadian mainland airspace — effectively the end of the transatlantic part of the flight.

The point PORGY is one of hundreds of worldwide navigation waypoints which are contained in the aircraft's Flight Management System (FMS) database. Again manufactured by Honeywell Sperry, the equipment's navigation database has a staggering one-million word capacity which is used to store the identification, position, and frequency (where appropriate) of all airfields, radio navigation aids and navigation waypoints within the aircraft's intended area of operation. For an aircraft like the 767 this implies a worldwide capability and the database is regularly updated so that all information is current.

Radio navigation aids are normally allocated a two or three-letter identification while airports all have a four-letter location indicator. Thus Prestwick is EGPK while Orlando is KMCO. Waypoints such as the Fish Points referred to above are given a five-letter designator and are arbitrary points which do not necessarily coincide with any specific feature at surface level.

Thus apart from PORGY, the other points along Canada's northeast coast include PRAWN, LOACH, SCROD and OYSTR. While there is some effort to ensure that the five-letter designator makes some sort of spoken word, such words are often meaningless but the FMS computer will immediately recognise them when entered on the pilot's keyboard.

In the operations office at Prestwick Ben plots NAT Track Alpha on his chart and also plots the parallel Track Bravo from the co-ordinates given on the AMR flight plan sheet. This is a routine check on the accuracy of his plotting as the routes shown should be parallel for most of the route, occasionally diverging at either side of the Atlantic. Normally Britannia pilots are required to plot the track on either side of their route as a double check but in this case, as the most northerly has been selected, it is only possible to draw in one other. Should the routes converge to less than 60nm apart, this would indicate an error in plotting or in the text of the telexed message laying down the route co-ordinates, and the whole plan would then be reviewed and checked.

The Track Alpha has been selected today to keep clear of a mid-Atlantic depression with an associated build-up of cloud and strong adverse winds. Once over Canada, and only halfway to Orlando, the AMR plan indicates a route coming overland to the St Lawrence Seaway and Quebec before turning south and passing well west of New York and Washington en route to Florida. This is intended to keep the aircraft well clear of a belt of violent thunderstorms with associated high level air turbulence which is sitting over the North American eastern seaboard.

Despite this favourable routeing a check of weather charts and the flightplan details shows that the aircraft will experience a steady headwind for most of the flight although this will become insignificant once over the North American continent.

The next stage in the preflight planning would be to draw up the aircraft's loadsheet which will determine the take-off weight of the aircraft once variables such as the passenger payload and the required fuel load are known. With these figures settled, the aircraft's take-off performance data can be checked so that the power ratings to be used and the various significant speed settings can be calculated. Unfortunately the Fax line to Britannia operations at Luton is playing up and the all important first page of the AMR plan which contains the vital fuel figures has not yet come through. In the meantime India Golf has arrived at Prest-

Above:

Above:
G-BRIG waits on the apron at Prestwick. Just behind the nose can be seen a vehicle with a raised body which is loading the considerable amount of catering supplies needed for the 283 people, passengers and crew, over the next 10hr.

complex automated aircraft like the Boeing 767, there is in fact little a pilot can check externally other than inspecting the aircraft for any signs of external damage, checking that engine exhausts and intakes are unobstructed with no damage to visible fan blades, and seeing that any doors and panels are closed and fastened.

wick and is parked on Stand 5 at the end of the passenger pier. In order to avoid delay, Captain Freeman elects to go out to the aircraft and begin the preflight checks while efforts continue to coax the recalcitrant Fax into parting with the urgently needed data.

Regrettably, air travel today is conducted in a state of semi-siege as governments, airlines and airports wage a never ending war against the threat of mindless terrorism. As a matter of course, anybody having access to the airside of an airport is required to undergo security screening and searching, and the flight crews are no exception — both Captain and First Officer therefore pass through the security gates, showing their airline identification passes and having their flight document cases thoroughly searched before being allowed to proceed to the aircraft. A small inconvenience of this procedure is that the outgoing crew will often not be able to speak to the crew from whom they are taking over as they pass into the terminal through a different channel.

Out on the apron, India Golf basks quietly in the sunshine, seemingly impervious to the bustle of activity preparing her for the flight to come. While Ben goes up the forward steps to the flightdeck, Graham carries out a walkround exterior inspection of the aircraft. With a large

Below:
A pre-flight check on the undercarriage. Modern undercarriage assemblies are amazingly small when the size of the aircraft is considered. A reduction in the size and weight of such components contributes to improving aircraft performance and payload characteristics.

Above:
This pump rig is used to feed fuel supplies from the airport's hydrant system into the single underwing refuelling point. The flow and distribution of fuel to the three aircraft tanks is controlled by an onboard computer which will cut off the flow when the preprogrammed amount has been loaded.

On completion of the external checks, Graham is met by the Scotex flight dispatcher who carries the final part of the AMR plan which shows the total fuel requirement to be 49,100kg, just over 49 tonnes. Once on the flightdeck he checks the entries in the aircraft's technical log against the reading on the tank gauges set into the overhead panel and confirms that the aircraft currently has just under 29 tonnes of fuel on board. He therefore advises the waiting aircraft refueller that a fuel uplift or 20,330kg is required.

Refuelling the 767 is a relatively straightforward procedure. Under the leading edge of each wing, outboard of the engine pylons, is a panel containing a hose connection point and controls for regulating the amount of fuel to be delivered. At Prestwick the fuel is contained in underground tanks beneath the apron with hydrants at each parking stand. A mobile refuelling rig, consisting of a pump and access gantry is positioned below the wing and connected to both the fuel hydrant and the aircraft's refuelling point. The operator then sets the required fuel uplift on a LED indicator in the underwing panel and opens the flow valve. The fuel is pumped into the aircraft's tank until the required quantity has been reached when the

aircraft's fuel control computer automatically shuts down the flow. The Jet A-1 Avtur fuel is stored in three main tanks, one in each wing holding approximately 18.5 tonnes each, and the remainder in the centre fuselage tank. Crossfeed pumps automatically distribute the fuel to the two wing tanks, only using the centre tank when the others are full.

Below:
Fuel Management is a vital part of the pilot's job and the controls are centrally mounted in the roof panel. Fuel quantities are shown (in tonnes) on the lower LED display. Should the quantities in each wing tank get out of balance, the FUEL CONFIG caption will light up, prompting the pilots to operate the pushbutton controls for the crossfeed pumps.

Britannia — BOEING 767 LOADSHEET
ALL WEIGHTS IN KILOGRAMMES

From	To	Flight No.	A/C Regn	Config	Crew	Date
PIK	MCO	316A	G BRIG	I/T 274	09	25.6.90

A.P.S.	INDEX	WEIGHT		ALLOWED TRAFFIC LOAD		
			MAXIMUM WEIGHTS	Zero Fuel	Take-off	Landing
Basic	+101	80335	FOR →	114758		126098
Galley	+9	2243	Take-off Fuel +	48800	Trip Fuel +	42180
1. 1M F/D	-1	80	Max. Allowed TOW − lowest of a, b or c	a) 163558	b) 154500	c) 168278
DRY OPERATING WEIGHT & INDEX	109	82658	Operating Weight −		131458	
Take-off Fuel (Ramp−Taxi)+		48800				
Ramp Fuel	49000		Allowed Traffic Load		23042	
Operating Weight	131458		Total Traffic Load		22177	
			Underloaded before L.M.C.		865	
			ACTUAL T/O		153635	
					154500	

NOTES
RUNWAY 31 FLAP 5
FULL PWR

Dest	No. of Pax.				Total	Cab. Bag. Wt.		Total		D e s t	WEIGHT DISTRIBUTION						Pcs. Chkd. Bag.
	M	F	C	I							1	2	3	4	5	0 Cabin	
B							B			B							
							C										
							M										
							T			A	NIL	641	1411	1413	100	NIL	282
A MCO	109 122 43 01				274+1 822												
Total																	

TRIM CALCULATION		
Item	Index −	Index +
Dry Op. Index		109
Hold 1	0	
Hold 2	4	
Hold 3		4
Hold 4		8
Hold 5	0	
Pax.	16	
Total	20	121
	−	20
ZERO FUEL INDEX		101
LMC ±		
TAKE-OFF FUEL INDEX	(+)	13
	+−	
TAKE-OFF INDEX		114

	B	3565
	C	—
	M	—
	T	3565
		822
Passenger Weights → +		17790
TOTAL TRAFFIC LOAD		22177
DRY OPERATING WEIGHT +		82658
ZERO FUEL WEIGHT		104835
Max Zero Fuel Wt. LMC ±		
114758 ±		
TAKE-OFF FUEL +		48800
ACTUAL TAKE-OFF WEIGHT		153635
Regulated TOW LMC ±		
154500 ±		
Trip Fuel −		42180
ESTIMATED LANDING WEIGHT		111455
Regulated LW LMC ±		
126098 ±		

Checked Pax/Baggage weights are **Actual** / AUTHORISED ESTIMATES

Maximum Weights For G-BKPW G-BKVZ:
Taxi	136984 kgs.
Take-off	136077 kgs.
Zero Fuel	112491 kgs.
Landing	122470 kgs.*

Maximum Weights For GBLKV GBLKW GBNCW:
Taxi	139252 kgs.
Take-off	138345 kgs.
Zero Fuel	113398 kgs.
Landing	123377 kgs.

Maximum Weights For G-BOPB G-BPFV G-BNYS G-BRIF (G-BRIG):
Taxi	157396 kgs.
Take-off	156489 kgs.
Zero Fuel	114758 kgs.
Landing	126098 kgs.

LAST MINUTE CHANGES

Item	Dest	Cpt	Weight ±	Index ±
Total Payload LMC				
Fuel ±				
TOTAL LMC				

TAKE-OFF C.G.
27 %M.A.C.
TOTAL PAX **274**

LOADING CERTIFICATE
I hereby certify that this aircraft is loaded in accordance with the current Loading Instructions of Britannia Airways Ltd.

Signed ....
Date ....

CAPTAIN'S CERTIFICATE
I hereby certify that I am satisfied this aircraft is loaded in accordance with the current loading instructions of Britannia Airways Ltd.

Captain _Freeman_
Date 25 JUNE 90

767 1 MARCH 90

In flight, each engine normally draws fuel from its wing tank which is continuously replenished from the centre tank until that is empty. The wing tanks are then gradually emptied for the remainder of the flight. The fuel computer continuously monitors fuel flows and quantities and will transfer fuel between the wing tanks in order to maintain equal amounts in each to keep the aircraft trimmed. In the unlikely event of an engine shutdown in flight, crossfeed pumps will supply the remaining engine from both wing tanks.

As the pilots board the aircraft they are met in turn by Alicia McMorley, the Senior Stewardess onboard and in charge of six other cabin staff who will be responsible for the care of the 273 passengers for the next 9hr. At the moment there are only the 63 passengers who have embarked at East Midlands and who stay on board while the aircraft is turned round at Prestwick.

The two pilots now settle down to a concentrated session of necessary but time-consuming preflight preparation. With the fuel load now known and the final passenger and baggage weights now available from the dispatcher, the Captain busies himself with completion of the aircraft's load sheet. Passenger load totals 17,790kg while cabin and hold baggage weighs in at 4,287kg — total payload of 22,077kg which in turn means that the aircraft's Zero Fuel Weight will be 104,735kg. With 49 tonnes of fuel on board, the aircraft will weigh in at 153,735kg and, allowing 200kg of fuel for start-up and taxying, take-off weight will be 153,535 tonnes — well within the certified 175,540kg maximum take-off weight.

Information from the loadsheet is used to calculate the aircraft's centre of gravity and trim setting for take-off. Both these values must be within laid down limits, otherwise the aircraft may be seriously out of trim, possibly to the extent of being uncontrollable. By consulting various tables the Captain determines a trim index, which can be plus or minus, for each part of the load. This included the five holds as well as the passenger and fuel loads. A final index of plus 114 is entered on to the loadsheet graph against the take-off weight. This shows the C of G to be at 27% MAC (Mean Aerodynamic Chord) and this falls nicely into the middle of the allowable range.

Using the loadsheet weight figures, Graham moves on to calculate the performance data for take-off. Ben has already selected frequency 127.125Mhz on his VHF radio panel in the centre console between the pilots so that he can listen to the continuous broadcast put out by the Prestwick Automatic Terminal Information System (ATIS). This gives weather and operational data for the airport and is updated every 30min. The current broadcast follows a standard format.

Prestwick ATIS: 'This is Prestwick ATIS Information Oscar. Runway in use Three One ILS serviceable. Taxiway links November and Papa are closed. Surface wind Two Niner Zero One Eight. Visibility greater than One Zero Kilometres. Four Okta Three Three Zero Zero Feet. Temperature Plus One Six. Dew Point One One. QNH One Zero One Seven. Report Information Oscar copied on first contact.'

Left:
Loadsheet for Flight BAL316A.

Right:
Despite the sophistication of the aircraft's computerised systems, there is still much of the traditional paperwork to be done before departure. The Captain is busy working through the complex loadsheet to determine the aircraft's take-off weight, centre of gravity and trim settings.

The Captain is particularly interested in the Runway in use, predictably the northwest-facing Runway 31 in view of the westerly wind, and wind and temperature data. Taking the aircraft's performance manual he turns to the pages giving information on departures from Runway 31 at Prestwick. Interpolation through columns of figures shows him that in the prevailing conditions and given the aircraft's weight he must use full power and 5° of flap.

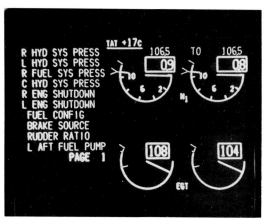

Above:

The upper EICAS prior to engine start-up. The top gauges show N1 fan speed and the lower the exhaust gas temperature. Note that readings are given in both analogue and digital form. On the left are various warning captions which should extinguish as the engines are started.

In some circumstances full power is not required and the manual contains columns of figures relating to take-offs with 8% and 17% reductions from full power. These settings are known as Derate 1 and Derate 2 respectively and are used wherever possible to help prolong engine life. Unfortunately the take-off weight today is just over that which would permit a Derate 1 take-off and so full power is required, although an option exists for what is termed an assumed temperature derate. On older aircraft the take-off power setting would be achieved by setting a 'bug' at the appropriate point on the scale of either an EPR (Exhaust Pressure Ratio) or N1 (fan speed) gauge and manually operating the throttles on take-off so that the pointers lined up with the bugs.

The 767 is different. A glance at the instrument panel in front of the pilots reveals that the previous standard confusing rows of conventional engine instruments have been replaced by two VDU screens of the Engine Indication and Crew Alerting System (EICAS) mounted one above the other in the centre of the panel where they can be monitored by either pilot. On these screens appear simplified graphic representations of the engine instruments which the EICAS has replaced. On the top screen are displayed the N1 and EGT (Exhaust Gas Temperature) readouts while N2 (engine core speed) and fuel flow are shown. In each case an exact digital readout is given as well as a pointer and scale representation. The lower screen also displays oil pressure and temperature, oil quantity and vibration indicator.

Using the keyboard of the FMC's Control and Display Unit (CDU) the Captain enters the take-off performance data and the required N1 setting then appears on the EICAS screen along with a pointer on the appropriate point of the circular scale. The aircraft's autothrottle system will ensure that the correct power settings are achieved on take-off. The thrust management control pushbutton control panel is just to the right of the upper EICAS display and pressing TO (Take-Off) will put the autothrottle system into the correct mode. For a Derate 1 or 2 take-off, the appropriate button (1 or 2) would also be pressed.

In fact, as will become apparent, much of the operation and flying of the aircraft is carried out by means of the CDU keyboard. While the Captain has been carrying out the external checks and his other preflight preparations, one of Ben's first tasks has been to check that the FMC is correctly set up and programmed for today's flight. The CDU screen, like most computer interfaces, is menu-driven and presents data and information in a series of 'pages'. On selecting the first page the First Officer can check that the database contained in the FMC covers the route to be flown and has been fully updated. Using the CDU keyboard he then enters the flight number, and the codes for Prestwick (PIK) and Orlando (ORL), enabling the computer to load the flight plan details. In many cases, keying in a further prompt will cause a standard preplanned route to be displayed. For example the code PIK5710 would show a standard routeing from Prestwick to entry of the OCA at point 5710N and thence to Bangor in Maine, USA. However, at present there is no preplanned route and consequently one must be entered manually. Before this can be done it is necessary to find out the departure routeing from Prestwick, known as the Standard Instrument Departure (SID), and confirm the Oceanic routeing. At this stage the ATC routeing over Canada and the United States can be disregarded and will be

EGPK

Trans alt **6000**		

1. Max IAS 250kt below FL100 unless otherwise authorised.
2. Initial climb: Ahead to 570.
3. Cruising levels will be allocated after departure by Scottish Control.
4. A/C unable to achieve altitudes at SID Termination Fixes must inform ATC before departure.

G1	lӘ

07 MAY 90

NOT TO SCALE

```
 4o   3₄
 3₉   3₈
```

SSA 25nm

FULMA
TRN 14d
TMA Bdy
N55 30·4
W005 00·0

FUL 1E
above **4400**

FUL 1F

GANET
TRN 9d
TMA Bdy
N55 23·5
W005 00·0

GAN 1E
above **4400**

HERON
TRN 8d
TMA Bdy
N55 20·6
W005 00·0

HER 1E
above **4400**

HER 1F

L
'PW' 277
N55 32·7
W004 40·8

13 MM

FUL 1E

255°

225°

GAN 1E
HER 1E

TRN 346R

TRN 330R

14
335°
9
310°
8
292°

'PW' 045M

25nm

L
'PE' 336
N55 28·2
W004 28·5

246°

FUL 1F
GAN 1F
HER 1F

above **4500**

TURNBERRY
'TRN' 117·5/355
N55 18·8
W004 47·0

SID	R/W	ROUTEING (including Min Noise Routeing)	ALTITUDES
FUL 1E	31	Ahead until past 13MM then left on Tr 255M('PW' 075M). At TRN 346R right to intercept and follow TRN 335R to FULMA. (Accel alt 3200).	FULMA above 4400 To 5000
FUL 1F	13	Ahead to L'PE' then right onto Tr 246M(TRN 066R) to TRN. At TRN right on TRN 335R to FULMA. (Accel alt 1400).	TRN above 4500 To 5000
GAN 1E	31	Ahead until past 13MM then left on Tr 225M('PW' 045M). At TRN 330R right to intercept and follow TRN 310R to GANET. (Accel alt 1400).	GANET above 4400 To 5000
GAN 1F	13	Ahead to L'PE' then right onto Tr 246M(TRN 066R) to TRN. At TRN right on TRN 246M(TRN 066R) to TRN. At TRN right on TRN 310R to GANET. (Accel alt 1400).	TRN above 4500 To 5000
HER 1E	31	Ahead until past 13MM then left on Tr 225M('PW' 045M). At TRN 310R right to intercept and follow TRN 292R to HERON.	HERON above 4400 To 5000
HER 1F	13	Ahead to L'PE' then right on Tr 246M(TRN 066R) to TRN. At TRN right on Tr 292R to HERON. (Accel alt 1400).	TRN above 4500 To 5000
		Min Noise Routeing for all SID's ends at 3000.	

Rev: Facility

© BRITISH AIRWAYS *AERAD*

Chart showing the FULMA Standard Instrument Departure (SID) from Prestwick. *Aerad*

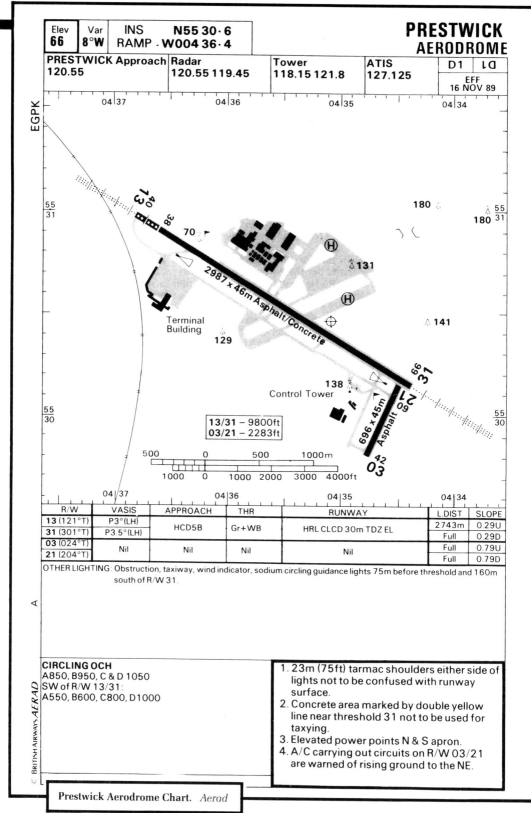

Elev	Var	INS	N55 30·6		PRESTWICK
66	8°W	RAMP -	W004 36·4		AERODROME

PRESTWICK Approach 120.55	Radar 120.55 119.45	Tower 118.15 121.8	ATIS 127.125	D1	ᒐᗡ
				EFF 16 NOV 89	

EGPK

180 ⋀ ⋀ 180

2987 x 46m Asphalt/Concrete

70 ▶

70

⊕ (H)

⊛ 131

(H)

Terminal Building

⋀ 129

⋀ 141

138

Control Tower

⊕

66 31

N 09

696 x 45m Asphalt

42 03

13/31 – 9800ft
03/21 – 2283ft

500   0   500   1000m
1000   0   1000 2000 3000 4000ft

R/W	VASIS	APPROACH	THR	RUNWAY	L.DIST	SLOPE
13 (121°T)	P3°(LH)	HCD5B	Gr+WB	HRL CLCD 30m TDZ EL	2743m	0.29U
31 (301°T)	P3.5°(LH)				Full	0.29D
03 (024°T)	Nil	Nil	Nil	Nil	Full	0.79U
21 (204°T)					Full	0.79D

OTHER LIGHTING: Obstruction, taxiway, wind indicator, sodium circling guidance lights 75m before threshold and 160m south of R/W 31.

A

CIRCLING OCH
A850, B950, C & D 1050
SW of R/W 13/31:
A550, B600, C800, D1000

1. 23m (75ft) tarmac shoulders either side of lights not to be confused with runway surface.
2. Concrete area marked by double yellow line near threshold 31 not to be used for taxying.
3. Elevated power points N & S apron.
4. A/C carrying out circuits on R/W 03/21 are warned of rising ground to the NE.

Prestwick Aerodrome Chart. *Aerad*

entered at a later stage when airborne. Normally, Oceanic clearances are received in the air after take-off as there is normally up to one hour's flight time before entering the OCA. However, departing from the west coast of Scotland leaves little time for this and consequently Oceanic clearances are requested from Shanwick on VHF while on the ground.

Reaching down to the VHF radio controls on the centre console, the First Officer selects frequency 123.95Mhz and calls the Oceanic Area Control Centre (OACC) at Redbrae, only a few miles north of Prestwick Airport.

First Officer: 'Shanwick Delivery, this is Britannia Three One Six Alpha requesting Oceanic clearance. Estimating Five Eight West, One Zero North at One Three One Zero. Requesting Flight Level Three Five Zero, Mach decimal Eight Zero.'

This request receives a short acknowledgement.

Shanwick: 'Britannia Three One Six Alpha, Shanwick. Roger, standby.'

The OACC will already have received a teleprinter signal initiated by Britannia Airways Operations at Luton giving the flight plan details as set out on the AMR plan. The controller at Redbrae considers whether it is possible to clear the aircraft along its requested route now that he has an idea of what time it will enter the OCA and can see what other aircraft are already airborne, also looking for clearances along the various NAT Tracks.

While awaiting their Oceanic clearance the two pilots continue with their preflight checks. The time is now 1310 (Local) but in aviation all reference to timings is done with respect to what is termed Universal Co-ordinated Time (UTC) which is just another name for Greenwich Meantime (GMT), UTC is used on a worldwide basis and is displayed on the aircraft's clock set in the lower right hand side of the Captains' instrument panel. Currently it is 1210 UTC and all references to time in the remainder of this book will be in respect of UTC unless otherwise indicated.

Using the aircraft weights and engine power settings already calculated, Captain Freeman continues to consult the aircraft performance tables to determine the important reference speeds to be used during the take-off. The first, V1, is the speed beyond which the pilot will continue with a take-off even if he should experience an engine failure or loss of power in one engine during the take-off ground roll. If he has not attained V1, he can abandon the take-off and bring the aircraft safely to a stop within the remaining runway available. VR is the speed at which the pilot will pull back on the control column to rotate the aircraft into a flying attitude and V2 is the minimum speed at which the aircraft can be safely controlled while climbing on one engine. Considering the aircraft's weight, the ambient air temperature, surface wind speed and direction, and engine power settings, the resulting speeds work out at 142kt V1, 155kt VR and 158kt V2. Graham then sets these speeds on his ASI by moving white plastic pointers ('bugs') to the appropriate points on the circular scale. Having done this he confirms the figures to the First Officer who also sets up his own ASI, cross-checking with the Captain's instrument.

In the meantime Ben has checked the Prestwick departure charts to find the Standard Instrument Departure (SID) appropriate for a climbout to the northwest. From Runway 31 this will be a FULMA 1E Departure which involves a left turn shortly after take-off on to a track of 255° which is maintained until a right turn is made on to a track of 335° as defined by a bearing, or Radial, from the Turnberry VOR — a radio beacon some 12 miles south of Prestwick. Once established on this track the aircraft will cross point FULMA when 14 miles distant from Turnberry. FULMA is to be crossed above 4,400ft altitude and the aircraft is to level off at 5,000ft unless cleared for further climb by ATC.

After FULMA the aircraft will continue on a northwesterly heading to cross the Benbecula VOR en route to the OCA entry point at 5810N. It is approximately 150nm to Benbecula and a further 124 miles to the OCA entry point. Ben busies himself setting these headings and routes into the FMC and also programmes in the flight-plan waypoints for the transatlantic crossing in anticipation of being cleared on Track Alpha. In fact while he is doing this Shanwick calls on the VHF to advise that it is ready to pass the Oceanic clearance. Before telling them to go ahead, Ben ensures that the captain is monitoring the transmission so that both pilots can cross-check the details.

First Officer: 'Go ahead with the clearance, Britannia Three One Six Alpha.'

Shanwick Delivery: 'Roger, Britannia Three One Six Alpha is cleared Track Alpha at Flight Level Three Five Zero, maintain Mach decimal Eight Zero, depart not before One Two Five Zero.'

It is normal practice for pilots to read back any ATC clearance and an additional requirement in this case is to include all the co-ordinates of Track Alpha to ensure that the NAT Track has been correctly plotted.

First Officer: 'Roger Shanwick, Three One Six Alpha is cleared Five Eight North One Zero West, Six Zero North Two Zero West, Six Zero North Three Zero West, Six Zero North Four Zero West, Five Eight North Five Zero West, PORGY. Maintain Three Five Zero Mach decimal Eight Zero. Depart not before One Two Five Zero.'

The readback is acknowledged and both pilots now double-check that the correct co-ordinates have been entered in the FMS. The restriction on the departure time is to ensure that the aircraft arrives at the OCA entry point (5810N) suitably separated from the previous aircraft at the same level. As the time is now 1221, this restriction presents no problem as the Prestwick passengers are still boarding and there are a few more tasks to complete before calling for start-up clearance.

At the rear of the centre console is a small data entry panel with an LED display. Known as the Aircraft Integrated Data System (AIDS) this can be used to access the FMC computers and display any of the parameters stored therein. It is normal practice to call up track miles to run to destination and total fuel used. This is done and shows a total of 3,7454nm and zero fuel used. The fuel readout will provide a useful check against the fuel remaining indications in the overhead fuel management panel.

As the pilots complete their paper work and are ready to begin their before start checks, the Dispatcher comes on to the flightdeck to confirm that all passengers and their baggage are on board and that the ground engineers are ready for pushback and engine start. After a final consultation to confirm the figures on the aircraft's loadsheet the Captain releases copies of the flight documentation to the Dispatcher for retention by the handling agents. This is a legal requirement as the information contained on these sheets may hold vital evidence in the unlikely event of an accident. With a cheery 'have a good trip', the Dispatcher leaves the aircraft, the last set of steps are withdrawn and the cabin crew close the doors. The time is 1236.

Captain Freeman now calls for the Pre-Start Checks. Each pilot checks his oxygen supply, the cabin signs (Fasten Seat Belts/No Smoking) are switched on, flight instruments are checked and the QNH set on each altimeter, parking brake is checked ON, fuel control levers for each engine are in CUTOFF position, flight recorder has been SET with flight number, time and date, and all locking pins and covers have been removed and are accounted for.

Moving on, the fuel quantity readings are checked and confirmed against calculated required fuel — on landing there should be 8.4 tonnes remaining which is enough for almost two hours' flying at cruising level. The ASI and N1 bug values are checked and the CDU is set to the first page of the route information.

For this flight the Captain has elected to fly the aircraft and is designated PF (Pilot Flying). Logically the First Officer therefore becomes PNF (Pilot Non-Flying) and will be responsible for all ATC and other air-to-ground radio procedures, checking and recording engine and fuel states, obtaining weather reports and generally monitoring the action of the PF. With all the take-off data calculated, the departure procedures and transatlantic routeings confirmed, Capt Freeman is now ready to run through the all important Departure briefing which covers the actions he will take in various emergency situations together with the supporting action he will expect from his First Officer.

The briefing covers the fact that this will be a full power take-off from Runway Three One with a FULMA 1E SID and he confirms that in the event of an engine failure before V1 he will call for the throttles to be fully retarded, speed brakes to be extended and full wheel-braking and reverse thrust to be applied. After V1 the take-off will be continued and standard drills instituted after gear up, depending on the actual nature of the emergency. Unless absolutely unavoidable, a return to Prestwick will not be made but the aircraft will divert to Glasgow where better engineering facilities are available and there will be time to burn off fuel to bring down the aircraft weight. In fact the 767 is certified to land at maximum take off weight, given a vertical descent of 7ft/sec compared with up to 10ft/sec at normal landing weights, and fuel dumping would not normally be required in an emergency. Safety altitudes within 25 miles of Prestwick are confirmed as being between 3,400 and 4,000ft, depending on the sector. Transition altitude is 6,000ft.

After the briefing is completed, the trim setting is checked against that shown on the loadsheet. Finally the flying controls are checked for correct operation. With all paperwork and checks completed, India Golf is ready to go. The time is 1247.

Departure

While the pilots have been working through their pre-flight routine, there has also been a rush of activity outside the aircraft. The last bags have been loaded, holds closed and secured, the refueller has completed his work and moved away, and all doors have been secured while the yellow painted access stairs are towed away. Out of sight below the nose, a tractor and towbar have been connected to the nosewheel assembly and an engineer plugs his headset into the aircraft's intercom using a socket conveniently adjacent to the nosewheel oleo. His report that all is ready for starting is the cue for Ben, the First Officer, to contact ATC for start-up clearance. Selecting frequency 118.15 on his VHF box he presses the transmit button on the control column. The time is 1248.

First Officer: 'Prestwick Tower, Britannia Three One Six Alpha request push back and start-up.'

Prestwick Tower: 'Britannia Three One Six Alpha push back and start approved. Temperature One Six.'

This clearance is acknowledged and the Captain immediately informs the ground engineer on the intercom that he is ready to start engines and that the brakes are released. With a slight jolt the tractor begins to push the 154 tonnes of aircraft slowly backwards from its parking stand while Graham reaches up to the overhead panel to initiate the engine start procedure. As with most modern jet aircraft, this is a simple exercise. Each engine has a mode selector switch and this is turned to the AUTO position while the single engine start switch is turned to 2. As the starboard engine spools up the core turbine speed (N2) comes up on the lower of the centrally-mounted EICAS displays, the readout being both digital and analogue, expressed as a percentage of the theoretical maximum rpm. As N2 passes 25% the HP fuel cocks, situated on the centre console immediately behind the thrust levers, are moved to the open position. With the latter set in the ground idle position the CF6-80A engine quickly stabilises at a fan speed (N1) around 23%. an exhaust gas temperature (EGT) of 380°C and N2 at just over 60%.

Fuel flow at this setting is 600kg/h. N1 and EGT readings are displayed on the upper EICAS while the N2 and fuel flow readings, together with indications of oil temperature, pressure and quantity are all shown on the lower display.

The port engine is started in similar manner, turning the start switch to 1, and with both engines running smoothly the After Start Checks are called out by the First Officer reading from his checklist.

First Officer: 'Engine anti-ice.'
Captain: 'Off.'
First Officer: 'Left and right isolation switches.'
Captain: 'Off.'
First Officer: 'Recall.'
Captain: 'Checked.'

This latter item is related to the EICAS displays. At various stages of the flight the upper display may show various captions and sound an alarm to draw the pilots' attention to the status of various aircraft systems. Warnings can range from

Below:
The EICAS display after engine start. N1 speed is around 24% and the EGT approximately 400°C. Note that all engine warning captions have been extinguished, leaving a reminder that the parking brake is still applied.

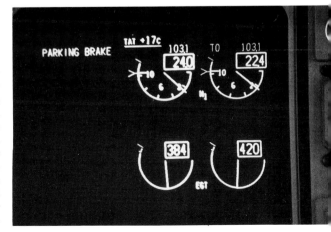

Above:
Aerial view of Prestwick Runway 31. *BAA Prestwick*

dire emergencies such as an engine fire to routine matters such as flap positions or cabin temperature settings. Emergency conditions requiring immediate action are shown in red while other conditions are shown in yellow and can be deleted from the screen if thought not to require any immediate action. Pressing the RECALL button during a checklist will cause any such deleted warnings which have not been actioned to reappear as a reminder.

With both engines started and the 767 pushed out on to the taxiway, the tractor is disengaged and the engineer reports that it has moved clear. This is confirmed by a visual check from the flightdeck and the Captain thanks the engineer for his help before the latter disconnects his headset and walks clear, giving a traditional thumbs up sign to indicate that the aircraft is clear to move. Ben now lets ATC know that they are ready.

First Officer: 'Prestwick Tower, Britannia Three One Six Alpha Heavy is ready to taxy.'

The addition of the word 'Heavy' to the callsign acts as a reminder to ATC that they are dealing with a large wide-bodied aircraft and, due to the wake turbulence created by such aircraft, will need to apply extra separation distances to smaller aircraft flying behind. Thus where aircraft under radar control are routinely kept three or five miles apart depending on circumstances, up to eight miles separation is called for when a smaller aircraft such as a BAe146 is following a wide-bodied aircraft. Prestwick immediately acknowledges the aircraft's call.

Prestwick Tower: 'Britannia Three One Six Alpha Heavy taxi to Hold Romeo for Runway Three One. QNH One Zero One Six. FULMA One Echo departure to destination. Squawk Seven Four One Four.'

Ben scribbles frantically on the margin of his flight log as he notes down these instructions and acknowledges their receipt.

First Officer: 'Roger. Hold Romeo, Runway Three One, One Zero One Six, FULMA One Echo, Squawk Seven Four One Four, Three One Six Alpha!'

Both pilots automatically scan the ground ahead and on each side of the aircraft, checking that all is clear. Graham releases the brakes and nudges the thrust levers very slightly forward to get the big 767 moving, almost immediately reducing power again to ground idle as the residual thrust is enough to keep the aircraft rolling smoothly down the taxiway which runs parallel to the main runway. Hold Romeo is at the far eastern end of the airfield, over a mile from the main parking apron, so the several minutes taxiing involved gives plenty of time to run through the pre take-off checks.

Right:
The undercarriage lever is positioned to the right of the EICAS displays, the three indicators above showing that all three units are locked in the down position. Note the flap position indicator to the left with the pushbutton autothrottle controls above.

Below:
A view from the First Officer's seat as the 767 moves slowly down the taxiway towards the runway. Prestwick's control tower is visible to the right.

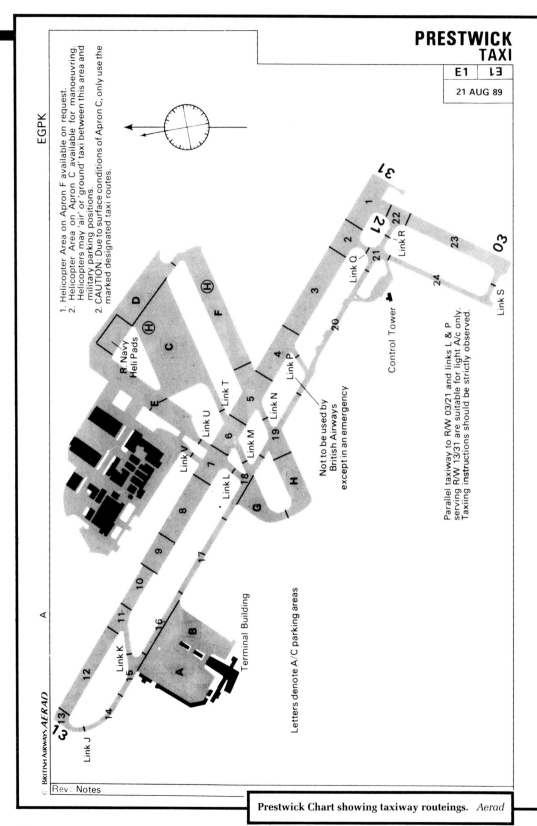

1. Helicopter Area on Apron F available on request.
2. Helicopter Area on Apron C available for manoeuvring. Helicopters may 'air' or 'ground' taxi between this area and military parking positions.
2. CAUTION: Due to surface conditions of Apron C, only use the marked designated taxi routes.

R. Navy Heli Pads

D

C

F

E

Link T

Link U

Link V

E

Link M

Link L

6

7

8

9

10

11

12

Link K

Link J

13

14

15

16

17

18

G

H

19

Link N

5

4

Link P

20

3

2

Link Q

21

Control Tower

Not to be used by British Airways except in an emergency

31

1

21

22

Link R

23

03

Link S

24

A

B

Terminal Building

Letters denote A/C parking areas

Parallel taxiway to R/W 03/21 and links L & P serving R/W 13/31 are suitable for light A/c only. Taxiing instructions should be strictly observed.

© BRITISH AIRWAYS AERAD

Rev: Notes

A

Prestwick Chart showing taxiway routeings. *Aerad*

34

Steering on the ground at taxying speeds is by means of this tiller which is positioned by the Captain's left knee.

First Officer: 'Flaps.'

The Captain reaches across to the flap lever to the right of the thrust levers and selects 5°, checking the readout on the flap indicator dial to the right of the EICAS screens before confirming, 'Five Degrees Set'.

First Officer: 'Packs.' (This refers to the aircraft cabin air conditioning packs controlled from the overhead panel.)
Captain: 'Packs on.'
First Officer: 'Autobrakes.'
Captain: 'Rejected take-off.'

As with everything else on this aircraft, nothing is as simple as it might appear. All modern aircraft are equipped with anti-skid units on the brakes to ensure that the wheels do not lock and lose adhesion, and in addition a selector switch to the left of the lower EICAS display can set up the degree of retardation which will result from application of the brakes. Normal landings, especially on long runways, call for only mild braking so a low retardation factor can be set which reduces brake wear and is more acceptable for the passengers. However in the event of a rejected take-off the aircraft will obviously require maximum braking effect and the RTO mode will provide this — although the amount of heat generated by the brakes often produce spectacular bursts of smoke.

While the 767 is taxying and the pilots complete their pre take-off checks, the cabin crew are seeing that all passengers are safely strapped in and the statutory safety briefing is in progress. On Britannia's modern 767 aircraft this is done by means of a pre-recorded video which is projected on a large screen at the front of each cabin section. This system enables a very detailed brief to be given in a manner which attracts the passengers' attention and a lot of vital information is packed into a few minutes' viewing. As soon as the briefing is completed and all seat belts have been checked, the Number One reports to the Captain that the cabin is secure and places a tag to indicate this in a slot on the panel immediately behind the co-pilot.

While the aircraft has been taxying, Prestwick ATC has contacted the Scottish Air Traffic Control Centre (ScATCC) at Redbrae, just north of the airport, to confirm the departure clearance for BAL316A. Having carried out the necessary co-ordination, Prestwick is now able to issue an amended departure clearance.

Prestwick Tower: 'Britannia Three One Six Alpha, after departure climb on heading three one zero. Maintain five thousand feet. Further climb when instructed by Scottish Radar.'

The First Officer acknowledges these instructions which effectively require the aircraft to maintain the runway heading after take-off instead of following the more complex FULMA 1E routine. This necessitates some resetting of the FMS and Autopilot controls. In anticipation of a direct routeing after departure, he keys in a track from Prestwick to the Benbecula VOR on the FMS keyboard. In addition he checks again that the correct frequencies have been set up on the VOR/ILS selectors mounted in the glareshield above the main instrument panel. The departure procedure is based on radials and distances from the Turnberry VOR (TRN), located some 12 miles south of the airfield, which transmits on 117.5MHz. Also selected is the frequency of the ILS for Runway 31 (110.30MHz) in case a return to Prestwick should be necessary. At this point the selection of radio navigation aid frequencies is entirely manual, but there is provision for an auto mode where the FMS will, based on its determination of the aircraft's position and stage of flight, automatically select the appropriate navaid frequency and display this information on the EHSI screen and FMS readout. This facility is normally selected once the aircraft is airborne and established on course.

The EHSI screen, selected in MAP mode with 80nm range displayed, currently shows the aircraft's position at the lower centre of the screen adjacent to the symbol denoting Prestwick's Runway 31. Across the top is an arc of the compass rose, in white, showing 30° either side of the aircraft's current heading of 129° as it proceeds down the taxiway. A white line stretches vertically up the centre of the screen giving a track reference and is marked off at 20-mile intervals while a triangular white symbol points to the aircraft's actual heading. The track which the aircraft is following at any given instant is shown in white figures immediately above the compass arc while a purple line shows the actual route which is programmed into the FMS computer. Scattered around the screen are a number of green symbols showing the position of various navaids within the 80-mile range set.

Finally the First Officer checks that the Flight Director system is on and functioning. This provides lateral and vertical cues from the FMS to the pilot through pointers on his EADI display and by following these he can manually fly the aircraft to the correct flight profile.

Apart from airline traffic, Prestwick Airport is host to the British Aerospace Flying College and several of its aircraft are in the circuit as the 767 makes its stately progress to the runway holding point, dwarfing the Piper Senecas and Warriors which form part of the college fleet. On the right, approaching the hold, is the rather soulless multi-storey Control Tower which has long since replaced the wartime tower perched on top of a converted cottage and which was a prominent feature of the airport in the heyday of piston-engined flying.

Despite the busy circuit, there is no delay to the Britannia flight's departure. After holding stationary for only a few seconds, while a Seneca sweeps over the threshold and lands, ATC is calling.

Prestwick Tower: 'Britannia Three One Six Alpha, line up Runway Three One.'

As the First Officer acknowledges, the Captain moves the thrust levers slightly forward, releases the brakes and swings round to the left to line up the big aircraft with the centre line markings of the runway. As he does so the EHSI display rotates although the aircraft symbol, coincident with the runway symbol, remains at bottom centre while the compass arc is now centred on 309°. The preset departure route to Benbecula is shown in purple, angled away to the northwest on a track shown as 331°.

A short pause as the Seneca ahead completes a touch and go on the runway and turns to the right as it climbs away.

Prestwick Tower: 'Britannia Three One Six Alpha cleared for take-off. Wind Two Three Zero at One Five Knots.'
First Officer: 'Britannia Three One Six heavy is rolling.'

A final scan of the EICAS shows no alert captions and all indications normal as the Captain calls for take-off power and, after pressing the Take-Off Mode button on the Thrust Management panel, Ben moves the thrust levers fully forward. Allowing a few seconds delay to ensure that engine power is building, the brakes are released and the 767 begins to accelerate

Below:
Runway Ahead! India Golf approaches the holding point for Prestwick's Runway 31.

Above:
Ready for take-off. The runway is clear ahead as ATC clears BAL316A to depart. The white markings either side of the centreline mark out 500ft intervals in the touchdown zone.

smoothly down the runway. Initially, steering is controlled by the tiller but, as speed builds the aerodynamic control surfaces, particularly the rudder, come into play rapidly.

First Officer: 'Eighty knots!'

By now the controls are fully effective and both engines are developing full power, confirmed by a glance at the EICAS screen which shows N1 at 103% against the purple bugs set by the FMS computer. Despite the 96,000lb thrust now being developed, the only indication of this immense power is a muted roar which blends with the increasing aerodynamic noise as the airspeed relentlessly increases, while force of acceleration presses crew and passengers firmly in their seats.

First Officer: 'Vee one.'

Ben watches the ASI and calls out the precalculated speeds as they occur. V1 has been set at 142kt and the aircraft, already more than halfway down the runway, in now committed to take-off. The white ASI needle continues to move clockwise around the scale.

First Officer: 'Vee R, rotate.'

155kt! The Captain eases the control column firmly back until the aircraft wings symbol on the EADI coincides with the horizontal Flight Director Command bar, thus achieving the correct angle of attack for the climb out. As the nose comes up the aircraft lifts cleanly away from the runway.

First Officer: 'Vee Two. Positive rate of climb!'

The two calls occur immediately after take-off, confirming that the single engine safety speed (158kt) has been attained and that the aircraft is climbing. The latter call also serves as a check that the VSI is functioning.

Captain: 'Gear Up.'

The First Officer moves the undercarriage lever to the UP position and watches as the indicator lights show red indicating 'Gear Unlocked' and then extinguish when all three units are retracted and the bay doors have closed. This is completed as the 767 passes 500ft.

Below:
Airborne. The Boeing 767 climbs away after take-off. Note the extension of the leading edge flaps.

Captain: 'Command. Heading hold.'

Up to this point Graham has been flying the aircraft manually, following the indications of the Flight Director on his EADI display. However, his latest instruction now calls for the First Officer to put the autopilot into COMMAND mode. Control of the aircraft now passes to the Automatic Flight Control System (AFCS — autopilot) which in turn operates on data received from the flight profile stored in the FMS. Ben presses the COMMAND button for the centre autopilot — there are in fact three separate autopilots — which is activated in the Heading Hold (HDG HLD) mode. This means that the aircraft will maintain its current heading and in addition the V/S (Vertical Speed) mode is also activated so that the current rate of climb (almost 4,000ft/min) will also be maintained.

Already the 767 is passing through 1,000ft and, having checked that the autopilot has correctly engaged, the Captain calls out another instruction.

Captain: 'Heading select, Three One Zero.'

This is intended to lock the aircraft on to the heading requested by ATC. The figure 310 has already been dialled up on the autopilot's heading selector and Ben now presses the HOLD button. In this instance there is almost no change of course as 310 virtually coincides with the runway heading. However, it is interesting to note that the rate of turn can be preset by selecting an angle of bank between 5° and 25°, but normally this control, in parallel with many others on this computer-managed aircraft, is left on the AUTO position. Passing 1,000ft altitude is also the marker for another event.

Captain: 'One thousand feet. Climb power.'

Control of the engines is via the autothrottles which, in turn, are activated through the FMS by means of the pushbutton Thrust Management control panel to the right of the upper EICAS display. For take-off the Take-Off/Go Around (TO/GA) mode has been selected which means that pushing the thrust levers fully forward has given full rated thrust for take-off. The Derate 1 and 2 thrust reductions, available for reduced power take-offs, are selected merely by additionally pressing the appropriate button marked 1 or 2. Pressing the CLB (Climb Power button) now means that the engines will run at a pre-determined power setting necessary to achieve the optimum rate of climb. Already cockpit noise has reduced when the nosewheel was retracted, giving less aerodynamic noise, and now a slight reduction in the engine note is detectable. The flightdeck routine is interrupted by a call from ATC.

Prestwick Tower: 'Britannia Three One Six Alpha airborne on the hour, contact Prestwick Radar One Two Zero decimal Five Five.'

Ben acknowledges, reading back the new frequency which he selects on his VHF radio, checking in with the Radar controller. One minute after take-off the aircraft is passing 2,000ft and speed is almost 200kt. The upper EICAS shows N1 at 99%, a slight reduction on take-off power.

Captain: 'Flaps up.'

The First Officer responds by moving the flap lever fully forward to UP and checks as the indicator needle moves round to the zero position. The limiting speed for 5° of flap is 220kt and, with the aircraft now in a clean configuration, speed continues to build past that figure. Time for the After Take-Off checks. Ben picks up the list and rattles off the calls.

First Officer: 'Landing gear.'
Captain: 'Up and off.'
First Officer: 'Flaps.'
Captain: 'Up.'
First Officer: 'Altimeters.'
Captain: 'Set and cross-checked'.

For the last check both altimeters are confirmed as set to the QNH value of 1017 millibars and a check made that both pilots' instruments give the same altitude readout on that setting (now 3,000ft). An altimeter, of course, works on the same principle as a barometer and indicates altitude by measuring the reduction in air pressure with increasing height. For the altimeter to give a correct altitude above sea level, the current sea level pressure (QNH) must be set on the instrument's subscale. At higher altitudes, a standard setting of 1013 millibars is set, the resulting altitude readout is then expressed as a Flight Level. As the altimeter check is completed there is another call from ATC.

Prestwick Radar: 'Britannia Three One Six Alpha contact Scottish Control One Two Seven decimal Two Seven.'

Above:

Three minutes after take-off, the instruments show the aircraft passing 7,600ft at a climb rate of 3,000ft/min. The EADI shows that the LNAV and VNAV autopilot modes are selected and speed is slightly above the bugged 250kt.

The call is acknowledged and Ben checks in on the new frequency, reporting that 4,000ft has been passed in the climb. More instructions are forthcoming.

Scottish Control: 'Roger Three One Six Alpha, Squawk Seven Four One Four Ident, No ATC speed restriction.'

On the instruction 'Squawk Ident' Ben presses the IDENT button on the transponder. The ground-based computer at ScATCC recognises the aircraft's code and causes the identity of the aircraft to appear on the controller's radar screen. At this point the aircraft is climbing within the Scottish TMA where a speed restriction of 250kt normally applies in order to ease ATC's workload. However, the controller can see that the aircraft's track is already passing clear of the busier parts of the TMA and is

happy to cancel this restriction. A few seconds later another call gives clearance to climb above 5,000ft.

Scottish Control: 'Britannia Three One Six Alpha continue climb to Flight Level Two Four Zero.'

Ben acknowledges this instruction, which has been passed just in time to prevent the aircraft levelling off at 5,000ft so that a continuous climb is achieved. He reaches up and winds the autopilot's altitude selector round to 24,000. With the initial departure routine completed the Captain now selects a further autopilot mode, reaching forward to press the button marked VNAV.

VNAV (Vertical Navigation) is run by the FMS through the AFCS and autothrottle and will ensure that the aircraft now climbs and descends along profiles calculated by the various computers as the most efficient for the flight. The exact degree of efficiency will in turn depend on the instruction keyed into the FMS while the aircraft was still on the ground. A normal flight profile would be a compromise between using as little fuel as possible while maintaining a reasonable speed along the route.

Factors taken into account include aircraft weight and configuration, weather data including winds and temperatures, distance to be flown and countless other variables. The required vertical profile is achieved by regulating engine power settings through the auto-throttles and adjusting aircraft attitude through the AFCS.

With VNAV selected, rate of climb drops back to just under 3,000ft/min and airspeed continues to build to around 255kt IAS. As the 767 passes through 5,000ft there is a broken layer of cloud but not enough to prevent the passengers catching glimpses of the Isle of Arran, below on the port side, and the Firth of Clyde stretching away to the north on the starboard side. ATC comes back with further instructions.

Scottish Control: 'Britannia Three One Six Alpha cleared own navigation direct Five Eight North Ten West.'

Until now the aircraft has been steadily maintaining the heading of 310°, as instructed by ATC on departure. Acknowledging the call, Ben reaches down to his FMS keyboard and enters 'RTE1 DCT 5810N'. As far as the FMS computer is concerned, the flight plan route entered prior to departure is Route 1 (RTE1) so that any amendments are treated as an alternative route until incorporated into the computer's memory. Having confirmed that DCT 5810N is now the required routeing, the FMS screen instructs Ben to EXECUTE which he does by pressing the appropriate button and the revision is now shown as part of RTE1.

On both pilots' EHSI display the purple line indicating the routeing now stretches out in a straight line on a track of 322°, displacing the previous line which showed a track of 335° to Benbecula and then a turn on to 301° for 5810N. However, instead of altering the heading selector to turn the aircraft, the Captain now selects his second main autopilot mode, LNAV — Lateral Navigation. At the same time he puts his VOR selector to AUTO. The aircraft will now follow the routeing automatically with the FMS using the triple inertial navigation platforms to continuously update position and making course corrections via the AFCS.

With the initial rush of the departure over, the crew can begin to relax a little as they monitor the aircraft's performance in the climb. In the passenger cabin the seatbelt signs have been automatically switched off (something else the aeroplane does for itself unless overridden manually) and the cabin crew are moving around

Above:

EHSI display at 1305, 5min after take-off. The aircraft's track is 322° but a 53kt crosswind is giving some 8° of drift. The arc at the centre of the screen shows the point at which the cleared altitude of 24,000ft will be reached, while T/C shows the point at which the cruising level of 35,000ft will be reached if ATC allows a continuous climb. Range from top to bottom of the screen is 160nm.

preparing to serve the first round of refreshments. Out of the seven cabin staff, one — the Number Five — is responsible among other duties for looking after the requirements of the two pilots. Linda now makes the first of many visits to the flightdeck with two welcome cups of coffee. In the nine hours ahead there will be plenty more cups consumed!

The Captain has now selected 160 miles range on his EHSI as the 767 banks to the right and comes round to a new heading to make good a direct track to 5810N. At the bottom left of the display a white arrow shows a crosswind component, from the left, while the figures 41 indicate the strength. To counteract this the autopilot settles on a heading of 314°. At top left a digital readout indicates 219 miles to 5810N while on the screen a small green circle indicates the point at which the aircraft will reach its planned cruising level (FL350), some 120 miles ahead. This is known as Top of Climb, abbreviated on screen to TC. At the moment the altitude selector is set at 240 — the limit of the ATC clearance — and a green arc shows that this level will be reached in another 30 miles.

Ten minutes after take-off, as the aircraft climbs out of the lower levels of Scottish Airspace, control is transferred to a High Level sector at ScATCC which looks after aircraft flying above FL240. Ben checks in on the new frequency, 124.05Mhz, and is immediately cleared to continue climb to FL310, this figure being set on the altitude selector. A minute later, a further call clears BAL316A all the way to FL350.

As the climb progresses, there are routine tasks to be accomplished. With the First Officer listening out on VHF for ATC instructions, the Captain reaches up and selects frequency 20065Hz on one of the two HF radios set into the overhead panel, making a check call to the British Telecom radio station at Portishead (near Bristol) to confirm that the set is functioning satisfactorily. He repeats this procedure with the second HF set.

At 1316 ATC calls, asking for an update on the aircraft's ETA for 5810N. Ben can read this directly off the route data displayed on the FMS screen and reports back.

First Officer: 'Scottish, Three One Six Alpha estimates Five Eight North One Zero West at Three Seven.'

Another routine check is carried out at this point on the navigation equipment. Once over the Atlantic the aircraft will rely entirely on its inertial platforms for navigation and it is therefore essential to carry out a practical check on the system. This is done by comparing the indicated bearing and distance from one or more VORs with the bearing and distance to the same VOR as calculated by the FMS using inertial data. The readings should be less than 4° apart in azimuth and less than four miles difference in distance when checked at a range of over 50 miles from the VOR. A series of key inputs to the FMS screen quickly throws up the required data and shows a discrepancy of less than one mile, an accuracy which is routine for this equipment. Should the inertial system be outside the required tolerances then the flight would not be permitted to continue across the ocean.

Cruising level (35,000ft) is reached at 1321, giving an average rate of climb since departure of just under 2,000ft/min, and position is some

100 miles northwest of Prestwick, over the sea to the southeast of the Outer Hebrides. The aircraft is now some four tonnes lighter, having consumed that amount of fuel during the climb. On reaching FL350 the autopilot has caused the 767 to level off and the autothrottles, now in Cruise mode, adjust power to maintain a speed of Mach 0.8 which equals 272kt IAS at this altitude. True Airspeed is almost 500kt. The engine readouts on the EICAS show N1 at 98.4% and an EGT of 707°C, and under these conditions the big-fanned CF6 engines are each swallowing just over two tonnes of fuel per hour.

Now in level flight with all engines and equipment functioning normally, India Golf is set up for the 2,000-mile Atlantic crossing. Indeed, with the battery of computers now running the aircraft, it is capable of flying all the way to Orlando along the correct route and at the appropriate altitudes without any further human intervention!

Below:
Level at 35,000ft. This instrument gives an unambiguous digital readout, while one revolution of the pointer occurs for every 1,000ft of altitude change.

En route

Above:
A 767 cruises over the ocean.

As the Boeing 767 cruises smoothly at 35,000ft, the passengers on the port side of the aircraft have only the clouds and the sea to look at, but on the other side the Outer Hebrides are visible through gaps in the cloud. Nearest is the island of Barra with South and North Uist faintly visible beyond. The time is 1329 as the last part of the British Isles falls astern and only the empty expanse of the Atlantic Ocean lies ahead.

In making a long range overwater flight in a twinjet it is essential that the crew should have a continuously updated plan of action in the unlikely event of the failure of one engine. In practical terms this boils down to planning a route whereby the aircraft will always be within the laid down 138min flying time (2hr plus 15%) of a suitable and available diversion airfield. Once airborne it is necessary to determine which airfields fulfil this criteria and keep a check on weather reports to ensure that they remain available. All suitable diversion airfields are programmed into the FMS database and so at any time the crew can determine which airfield is the nearest in terms of flying time. At this stage of the flight the most obvious course of action would be to return to a UK airfield but, for example, interrogation of the FMS shows that Keflavik in Iceland is 547 miles away on a

track of 331° — approximately 100min flying time at the single-engine cruise speed of 497kt. Other possible alternatives will be Sondrestromfjord in Greenland, and Goose Bay and Gander on the eastern Canadian seaboard. Routeing this far north means that the aircraft will at all times be well within the 138min limit.

In the meantime the purple waypoint symbol for 5810N is creeping down the EHSI display and this position is crossed at 1336. BAL316A has now passed out of British airspace and is entering Shanwick Oceanic Control Area. Ben reports this fact to ScATCC who, by now, will be losing radar contact with the aircraft.

First Officer: 'Scottish, Britannia Three One Six Alpha is Five Eight North One Zero West at Three Six, Flight Level Three Five Zero.'

The call is acknowledged and shortly afterwards ATC transfers control to the OACC.

Scottish Control: 'Britannia Three One Six Alpha contact Shanwick on Four Six Seven Five or Eight Eight Nine One, goodbye.'

Ben now reaches up and selects the first frequency on his HF box. HF radio transmissions are much more subject to varying atmospheric propagation than short-range VHF and hence it is normal practice to have alternate frequencies available in case two-way contact cannot be established with one or the other. Today Shanwick comes over loud and clear and Ben is able to pass his first oceanic position report without much trouble. The format of these position reports has not changed since the days of piston-engined transatlantic flying, the only difference is that, today, aircraft are not expected to pass a mass of meteorological observations with each report. In the past, such weather reports provided vital data for the forecasters but much of this is now gained from the many weather satellites circling the Earth.

First Officer: 'Shanwick, Britannia Three One Six Alpha was Five Eight North One Zero West at One Three Three Six, Flight Level Three Five Zero, estimate Six Zero North Two Zero West at One Four Two Two, Six Zero North Three Zero West next.'

There is a short pause while the ground radio operator jots all this down before the HF crack-

Above:
On oceanic routes aircraft are required to fly at specified Mach numbers. In the cruise, the ASI shows a steady Mach 0.8 which translates to an Indicated Airspeed of 272kt. Correcting for temperature (−30°C) and altitude would give a True Airspeed of almost 500kt. The striped needle, known as the 'barber's pole', indicated the maximum permissible speed (Vmo) at this altitude.

les into life as he reads the figures back to ensure that the report has been received correctly. The crew will now not need to make another routine report for almost three-quarters of an hour. Communications between the aircraft and the OACC at Redbrae on HF are cumbersome by today's standards. In a hangover from the days when Shannon and Prestwick controlled different sectors of the OCA, the HF radio operators are situated at Ballygirren in Ireland and messages are sent to the controllers at Radbrae by discrete teleprinter network. Controllers' instructions are telexed to Ireland for onward transmission to the aircraft. In the near future it is expected that the old HF links will be replaced by a direct pilot controller voice link using a satellite communications system. Once this is in place, position data from the aircraft's navigation systems can be transmitted enabling a synthetic radar-type display to be compiled at the OACC. However, for the moment, the long-established HF network remains in place.

To avoid having to listen out for long periods to the hissing static on the radio, aircraft are fitted with a device termed 'Selcal' (Selective Call) whereby the crew can be alerted if the ground station wishes to make contact. The First Officer now proceeds to check that this is functioning.

First Officer: 'Shanwick Britannia Three One Six Alpha request Selcal check Echo Golf Kilo Mike.'

EGKM is the aircraft's Selcal code which is pre-set on installation of the equipment. As soon as the Shanwick operator has selected and transmitted this code, a two-tone gong sounds on the flightdeck and his voice is heard.

Shanwick OACC: 'Selcal check Echo Golf Kilo Mike, frequency Four Six Seven Five.'
First Officer: 'Selcal check OK, Selcal watch this frequency.'

Now that the flight is passing out of VHF range and is using the HF for routine communications, the lefthand VHF is set to 131.8MHz (used as a common frequency in the OCA for aircraft to talk to each other if required) and the righthand to 121.5, the international distress frequency.

With satisfactory communications established, the crew carry on with more flightdeck routine. To save time before departure, the FMS had only been programmed in detail as far as PORGY, the entry point to Canadian airspace. The two pilots now consult the flight and charts

Above:
The First Officer uses the CDU keyboard to update the route data in the FMS computer while the Captain checks off the waypoints from his flightplan.

to decide on the likely routeing to Orlando through Canadian and American airspace, entering the various waypoints via the FMS keyboard. A look at the Orlando arrival charts seems to indicate a BITHO 5 arrival pattern as being most likely and this procedure is also entered. Entering this data takes nearly 30min by the time each waypoint has been entered, checked and double checked. The FMS is like any other computer and reacts to the 'Garbage In, Garbage Out' syndrome, only in this case the results can be quite disastrous. For this reason the entering of route data is a carefully monitored procedure.

At 1412, while the First Officer is finalising the data input, the Captain again contacts Portishead on his HF box and requests a talkthrough to Britannia Airways Operations at Luton Airport. The British Telecom radio operator patches the HF through to the telephone network so that Graham can talk directly to the Duty Operations Officer at Luton. Once in contact the message is routine and brief.

Captain: 'Hello Operations, India Golf was off blocks at Prestwick at One Two Fife Zero. Two Seven Four passengers. Orlando at Two One Fife Zero. All serviceable.'

Once this is acknowledged, Graham calls up Portishead who will have been listening in.

Captain: 'Portishead, talkthrough complete. Request Selcal check Echo Golf Kilo Mike.'

Portishead responds with the check, which functions correctly.

Captain: 'Selcal OK. Selcal watch this frequency.'

It is now almost and hour-and-a-half into the flight and the passengers are being served the first of two meals. Linda looks in on the flightdeck to see if either of the pilots is ready to eat. On safety grounds the pilots will take their meals at different times so that one retains full control of the aircraft, and also they are required to choose from a menu of non-identical separately prepared meals and snacks in order to avoid any possibility of both being incapacitated by food poisoning. Ben elects to eat first and chooses a simple chicken salad with cheese and biscuits.

As he begins to eat, the aircraft passes position 6020N, some 250 miles southeast of Keflavik. The time is 1420 and Ben interrupts his meal to make the routine position report on the HF to Shanwick. On this occasion he prefixes his transmission with the words 'Copy Gander' which will alert the Canadian HF operator listening out on the frequency to pass the information on to the controller at the Gander

Above:
Details of the Captain's flight progress report are received here at the Britannia Airways Operations Centre, Luton. The Duty Officer has information on all the airline's flights displayed in front of him and is responsible for making plans to deal with any disruption caused by diversions, unserviceable aircraft, weather and other incidents.

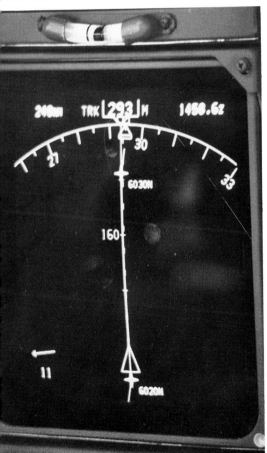

Left:
The EHSI display at 1456, just after passing 6020N. The aircraft's track is 293° and there are 240 miles to run to the next waypoint, 6030N.

OACC. This will enable them to update their flightplan data on the flight ready to accept control of the aircraft once it passes 30° West — roughly at the midpoint of the crossing.

The HF reception is becoming poor and after ensuring that his position report has been received he returns to the alternate frequency, 8891Hz. Finding reception much improved, he carries out a routine Selcal check and maintains a listening watch on the new frequency.

On passing 6020N, the autopilot brings the aircraft round to the left and steadies on a new heading of 294°. The engines have now consumed a total of 8,891kg of fuel, leaving just under 40 tonnes remaining. This is distributed between the two main wing tanks which are both full and hold 18.5 tonnes each while the remaining three tonnes is in the centre fuselage tank. Maximum fuel capacity on this aircraft is 50.8 tonnes made up of 37 tonnes in the two wing tanks and the remaining 13.8 tonnes in the centre. For flights requiring less than 37 tonnes, the centre tank is left empty but today it was filled to just below capacity at 11.8 tonnes. In flight the engines normally feed from their respective wing tanks which are kept full by a steady transfer from the centre tank. Once this is empty the wing tanks begin to drain but crossfeed pumps are used to ensure that the quantities in each wing remain approximately equal in order to avoid an unbalancing effect on the aircraft. Fuel management is kept simple with the three tank quantity LED readouts, plus fuel total and temperature, are displayed in the overhead panel. Just above are the manual controls for the crossfeed pumps although these are rarely used as the fuel management is, again, fully automatic and computer controlled. Any problems will be annunciated on the EICAS warning panel so that the crew can take any necessary actions.

The next 30min pass quietly. After finishing his snack and tidying the tray away, Ben takes out the aircraft's technical log from its stowage rack behind the centre console and notes down the current engine parameters (N1, N2, EGT etc). On long-haul flights this task is done approximately every two hours and enables the ground engineers to monitor the long-term performance of the engine and possibly anticipate any problems. Of course a continuous and detailed readout of engine and aircraft performance is available as a printout from the FMS at the end of every flight and this is retained with other flight documentation. However, this would only be used for detailed analysis and the technical log entries are normally sufficient for day-to-day monitoring.

The maintenance of the airline's fleet of Boeing 767 aircraft engaged on Extended Range Operations (EROPS) is a vital contribution to the safety and reliability of these flights. The British Civil Aviation Authority lays down the complex maintenance schedule to which the airline must adhere and also, in consultation with the operator, draws up a list of equipment which must be serviceable before the start of any EROPS flight. Once a pre-EROPS check has been carried out, it is valid for 24hr only and, if, within that 24hr the aircraft is to make a return flight in the opposite direction, then a further check must be satisfactorily completed. The EROPS check on India Golf for today's flight was carried out at East Midlands Airport and validated the aircraft for its sectors to Prestwick and onward to Orlando. Checks for the return flight will be carried out at Orlando by engineers from Delta Airlines who are under contract to Britannia Airways, saving the British airline the expense of maintaining its own staff in Florida.

In order to be certified for EROPS the aircraft and its equipment must meet certain criteria laid down by the CAA in their official publication, CAP513. The basic criteria is that the aircraft's engines must have shown a required level of reliability based on actual in-service experience over thousands of hours. If an engine should fail in flight, then the other engine will have to operate at a higher than normal rating for the remainder of the flight which could be in

Below:
EROPS flights demand a high standard of maintenance. A 767 is shown undergoing a major check at Britannia's Luton base.

excess of three hours. The engine manufacturer will therefore have to demonstrate during the certification programme that the engine is capable of doing this without degradation of performance or reliability.

The aircraft's systems depend entirely on the supply of electrical power from the two engine-driven generators. The loss of power from one engine would automatically halve the available electrical power and so, to meet EROPS criteria, Boeing has installed a third generator which is driven by a hydraulic motor powered from the aircraft's central hydraulic system. This HMG will start up automatically in the event of an engine failure and provides, among other things, an independent power supply for the Captain's flight instruments and FMS. In addition there is also the APU which is normally used to provide electrical power when the aircraft is on the ground.

As this aircraft is almost completely dependent on its avionic systems and computers it is essential that these remain fully serviceable. Most electronic systems are sensitive to overheating and the avionics bay in the nose has its own air conditioning system. Unserviceability of this equipment is a strictly 'No-Go' item on the preflight checklist.

Another problem which must be considered, although unlikely to occur, is the possibility of a fire in the cargo compartment. As the aircraft may have to fly for several hours before being able to land, a Cargo Fire Suppression Metering System is installed in all cargo bays. Basically this means that increased quantities of firefighting agents are carried and these can be deployed over a continuing period rather than as a single shot. On the Boeing 767-200ER this system has a 195min capability. In fact this system so much improves safety on overwater flights that it is becoming mandatory on all aircraft making long range overwater flights, not just the EROPS twinjets.

Back on the flightdeck, Ben calls Shanwick on HF to report crossing position 6030N at 1459 and passes a forward estimate for 6040N of 1538. The aircraft has now crossed the boundary between the Shanwick and Gander areas of responsibility in the OCA and accordingly, after copying the position report, the Shanwick operator instructs BAL316A to contact Gander Control. The new frequency is 11336Hz and Ben duly checks in with Gander and goes through the routine of setting up the Selcal listening watch.

By now the Captain is taking a few minutes relaxation and is nibbling at his snack meal, a beef and rice dish. By the time he has finished, the aircraft is almost exactly at the midpoint of its Atlantic crossing — a convenient point to update the passengers on the flight's progress. Selecting the cabin PA system on his communications box, Graham chats amiably for a few minutes, giving a provisional estimated time of

Below:
To accommodate the 767, a new hangar was erected at Luton in 1983. This was extended at a cost of £5 million in 1990 so that two aircraft could be accommodated simultaneously. In addition to its own aircraft, Britannia has carried out 767 maintenance work for a number of other airlines including Air Seychelles and Lauda Air.

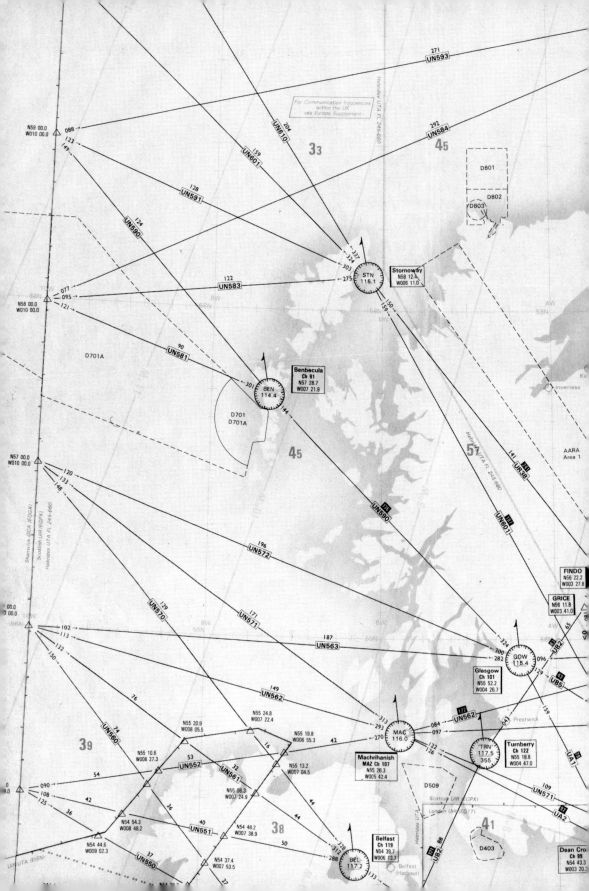

arrival for Orlando of approximately 2230
British Summer Time which will equate to 1730
Local time at Orlando — late afternoon.

Aboard the 767 the passengers can actually
follow the progress of the flight for themselves.
Using information from the FMS, a simplified
moving map display can be projected on to the
video screens on the forward bulkhead of each
cabin section. This is normally done when the
screens are not being used for showing the normal round of inflight entertainment which is
now standard on all long-haul flights.

Once communication with Gander has been
established, the crew now concentrate on picking up the latest weather reports from airfields
along the route. A whole range of reports and
forecasts is available on an HF network utilised
by New York, Gander and Shannon. On the
North American side the first two share a group
of four frequencies (3485, 6604, 10051,
13270Hz) which are allocated on a timeshare
basis. Thus, for example, on each frequency at
25min past each hour Gander transmits forecasts and actual reports for Montreal, Ottawa
and Toronto, followed by Winnipeg, Edmonton
and Calgary. At 30min past, New York transmits
details for Niagara, Milwaukee and Indianapolis.
While the Captain monitors the ATC HF link,
Ben selects 10051MHz and copies the 1520
transmission.

Gander reports overcast at 900ft, temperature
14°C, wind southwesterly at 8kt and a visibility
of 12 miles. Despite international agreements
intended to standardise aeronautical procedures, there are several points where the North
American subcontinent differs from practice in
other parts of the world. Weather report format
is one of these. For example, in most parts of the
world the amount of cloud is reported in eighths
of the sky covered (oktas), while visibility is
reported in metric units. In North America the
latter is given in statute miles while cloud is
reported as being overcast, broken or scattered.
There are also other subtle differences in the
meanings of various instructions issued by ATC
and consequently European crews have to be
fully briefed on these in order to prevent misun-
derstandings.

At 1539 the waypoint symbol for 6040N
passes under the white aircraft symbol on the
EHIS and the autopilot banks the aircraft to the
left as it swings round to take up a new track of
278°M. As the flight progresses westwards, it is
flying into the regions where there are marked
differences between the direction of the true and
magnetic North Poles. At this point the difference, or variation, is around 30°. The EHIS display is currently set up to show all headings and
tracks with reference to magnetic north and so a
track of 278°M is actual around 248° true,
approximately SSW. True tracks and headings
can be displayed if required.

As the aircraft settles on its new course, Ben
makes a routine position report to Gander and
then notes that a total of 15 tonnes of fuel has
now been used up. A little under 34 tonnes left!

On these long overwater sectors there is normally little to see except for the sea and sheets
of cloud, all a long way below. Looking ahead
there appears to be a long line of brilliant white
cloud on the distant horizon, just to the right of
the nose. A closer look now reveals this to be
the ragged eastern coastline of Greenland,
backed by high snow-covered mountains
stretching west and north as far as the eye can
see. The nearest point of the coast is almost 100
miles away, but as time passes the southern tip
of this great frozen land mass is less than 20
miles away on the starboard side. In mid-June
the sea here is free of ice and is a brilliant blue,
reflecting the deep hues of the sky. Some of the
valleys and lower slopes of the mountains are

Below:
**Midway across the Atlantic and the rugged coast of
Greenland is visible away to starboard. A layer of sea
mist lies offshore and the mountain peaks are visible
in the distance.**

Above:
Although it is midsummer, Greenland's landscape presents a forbidding sight from 35,000ft. The nearest airfield, Sondestrom, is 500 miles away.

free of snow and, even from 35,000ft, some signs of habitation are visible. Altogether it is a dramatic and thought provoking sight, and both pilots watch silently until a layer of cloud drifts on from the west, blanking out any view of the land. Sondrestrom, the only airfield in Greenland likely to be used as a diversion, lies some 500 miles away to the NNW.

In considering which airfields will be used as diversion destinations in the event of an engine failure, there are many factors to be kept in mind and the most important of these is fuel. In fact the choices are laid down in the AMR flight plan which calculates the Critical Point (CP) and Critical Fuel (CF) for each pair of diversion airfields. On today's flight the diversion options are listed as Prestwick or Keflavik for the early stages, and Keflavik and Goose Bay for the last two-thirds of the crossing. Taking into account forecast winds and aircraft performance, the flight plan shows that in relation to the second pair, the CP is 59°16'N 44°22'W — 678nm from Keflavik or 630 miles from Goose Bay. Before reaching the CP the aircraft would be obliged to turn back towards Keflavik in the event of an emergency, while after passing the CP it would

continue on to Goose Bay. The flight plan also shows that the CF is 11,457kg. Critical fuel is defined as the fuel required to reach the diversion airfield based on descent to 10,000ft, single engine cruise at 330kt, descent, one missed approach, circuit and landing plus 15min holding at 1,500ft. This figure is then increased by 12% to allow for possible airframe icing. On this flight the fuel remaining at the CP is calculated as 31,408kg, leaving a more than adequate margin over the CF required. On westbound flights where the overwater sector occurs first, this is usually the case. However, on eastbound flights there may be a shortfall between CF and fuel on board. If this is forecast then the Captain must ensure that the necessary extra fuel is loaded before take-off.

The cloud closing in below the aircraft is associated with frontal weather activity further south and although the present route keeps clear of the forecast areas of air turbulence, the aircraft is now running into headwinds of around 70kt. This slows progress and, although ground speed is still around 400kt it takes 50min to cover the 350 miles to the next waypoint at 5850N. Fuel burn off is now 18,661kg. Goose Bay airfield is 480 miles away to the SW and, despite the headwinds, is well within the required 138min flying time. The nearest point of the Canadian coast is actually less than 300 miles directly ahead and the pace of activity, which has been relaxed for the past three hours, begins to take on a brisker pace.

Left:
The transoceanic part of the flight is almost completed as the EHSI display shows that the aircraft has just passed the PORGY waypoint, 800 miles out from the Canadian coast. The arc in front of the aircraft symbol shows the point at which a change of level, to 39,000ft, should be instituted, and the circular symbol on the left of the screen is the position of Goose Bay airfield.

Ben acknowledges this and, thanking Gander for its assistance, switches over to his VHF radio and selects the new frequency. The aircraft is now some 20 tonnes lighter than when it took off, due to the amount of fuel used and the FMC readout indicated that a climb to 39,000ft would give improved fuel consumption for the remainder of the flight.

First Officer: 'Moncton Control, this is Britannia Three One Six Alpha Heavy estimating PORGY at One Seven One Zero, Flight Level Three Five Zero, requesting Three Nine Zero when available.'

Moncton Control: 'Britannia Three One Six

At 1700, with 10min to run to point PORGY which marks the boundary of the OCA, Gander calls up on the HF.

Gander Control: 'Britannia Three One Six Alpha, contact Moncton Control on One Three Five decimal Four.'

Below:
Ben minds the shop while the Captain takes advantage of a quiet period to stretch his legs.

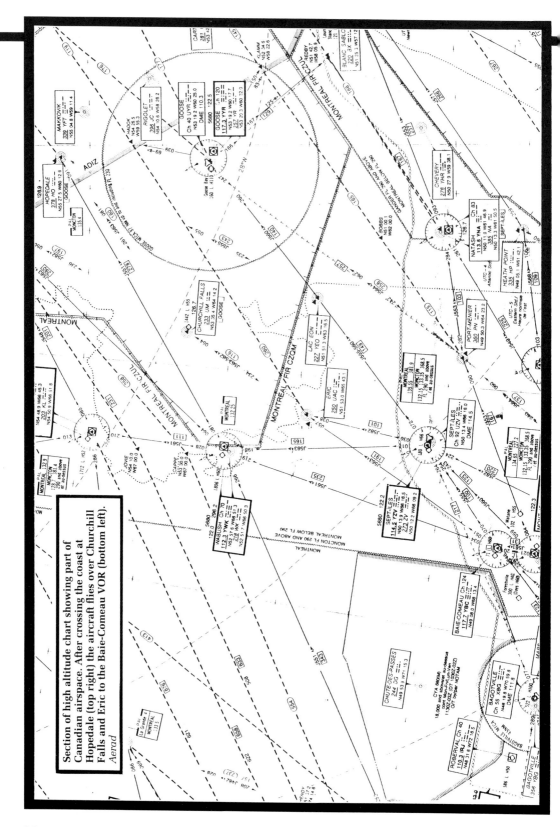

Section of high altitude chart showing part of Canadian airspace. After crossing the coast at Hopedale (top right) the aircraft flies over Churchill Falls and Eric to the Baie-Comeau VOR (bottom left).

Aerad

Alpha Heavy, Moncton Roger. Maintain Three Five Zero, report PORGY.'

At this stage the controller merely acknowledges this request as the aircraft must maintain its presently assigned level until clear of the OCA. PORGY is passed at 1710 and BAL316A is now in Canadian airspace with the long ocean crossing virtually completed. It has taken 4hr and 10min since departure from Prestwick but almost 5hr flying remains. The flight has barely reached the halfway point!

As soon as Ben reports passing PORGY, the controller advises that he is ready to pass the airways route clearance for the North American sector of the flight. Ben grabs his pencil and tells the controller to go ahead.

Moncton Control: 'Britannia Three One Six Alpha is cleared Hopedale Jet Five Six Three Baie-Comeau Jet Five Five Five Quebec Jet Five Six Zero Plattsburgh Jet Two Nine Syracuse Jet Five Nine Jet Seven Eight Charleston Jet Eight Five Jet Five Three Jet Four Five Orlando. Climb to Flight Level Three Nine Zero. Squawk Zero Seven One Three!'

Both pilots have been writing frantically as the controller rattles off this complex routeing without a pause. After comparing notes Ben reads the clearance back to Moncton to confirm that it has been correctly copied. The captain then winds the autopilot altitude selector to 39,000 in order to initiate a climb to that level. This is achieved in just under 5min and Ben reports level at FL390 at 1718. While in the climb, the Captain has checked the accuracy of the inertial reference system by obtaining a radial and distance from the GOOSE VOR, 140 miles to the south. The discrepancy between the two systems is less than a mile!

Attention now turns to the routeing specified in the ATC clearance. In the UK and Europe air routes or airways are designated by a letter and a number (eg, Golf One) and known as Upper Air Routes if above FL245 (eg, Upper Bravo Five). In the United States and much of Canada, the division between Upper and Lower airspace occurs at 18,000ft and airways above that are known as Jet Routes while those below are Victor Routes. Hence terms such as Jet 563 and Jet 79 refer to the airways to be followed.

After passing PORGY, some 90 miles offshore, the first en route fix is the Hopedale NDB situated on the Newfoundland coast and marking the start of Jet 563. From there the route leads southwest to the St Lawrence River, then over Quebec and Montreal, entering US airspace over New York State and following a course down the eastern US, some 200 miles inland from the coast. ATC has allocated this route in order to keep well clear of some intense thunderstorms and areas of turbulence associated with a frontal weather system sweeping up the eastern seaboard. The tops of some of the violent cumulas clouds associated with this activity are forecast to rise well above 35,000ft so the detour is well worthwhile. However it differs in detail from the standard route which had been expected and so, once the aircraft has levelled off at FL390, both pilots begin the task of checking the new route against the details already held in the FMS computer. While Ben works on his keyboard, the Captain calls out the waypoints and checks that they are correctly entered. Once this has been done, the whole route is then double-checked before being finally accepted by the FMS as the definitive version, supplanting the one previously held.

While this is being done, Hopedale is crossed at 1723, and the autopilot alters course slightly to maintain a track of 261° on Jet 563. Ben makes a routine position report to ATC, which is acknowledged, before continuing with his FMS input. This is completed just in time to hear a call from ATC instructing a frequency change to 128.7, another control sector at the Moncton ATCC. Next waypoint is Churchill Falls, located by an NDB, and marking the point where Jet 655 turns left on to a track of 234° for 116 miles before passing another NDB with the unlikely name of Eric and then continuing a further 191 miles to the Baie-Comeau VOR on the north shore of the St Lawrence River.

Just before reaching Churchill Falls, at 1744, Moncton calls up and clears BAL316A direct to Baie-Comeau giving a straight run for the next 300 miles. After the flurry of work involved in making the landfall and integrating into the Canadian ATC system the pilots can relax a little and take a look at the world passing below, In this they are joined for a while by a steady stream of passengers, mainly youngsters and their dads, eager to see what goes on. Years ago children visiting the flightdeck of an airliner would look in wonderment at the numerous dials, lights, switches and controls. It is perhaps an interesting sidelight of modern times that today's youngsters seem to take the advanced electronic display screens and computer-controlled autopilot very much for granted. It's just like a video game to them!

Far below, the clouds which had obscured the ground after crossing the coast are beginning to

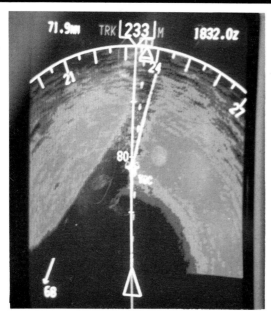

71.9нм   TRK ⌊233⌋M   1832.0z

Above:

A dramatic picture of the EHSI display showing 80 miles to run to the Baie-Comeau VOR. The weather radar has been switched on and the picture superimposed on the display. By tilting the aerial down the land mass and coastal features ahead can be seen. The dark area running from bottom left to top centre is the wide St Lawrence River which runs down to the Atlantic from the Great Lakes.

The sight of the countryside below prompts Graham Freeman to talk of his previous career as a pilot. Joining the RAF for his National Service in the 1950s, he was selected for pilot training and sent to Canada where he gained his wings. Taking a short service commission he remained in the RAF for eight years after which his love of flying and memories of his training in Canada led him to join the RCAF during the 1960s. After completing his term of engagement he returned to the UK and took up commercial flying, joining Britannia Airways in 1967. During his RCAF service he flew Grumman Albatross amphibians from the base at Trenton, Ontario, and often landed on the stretches of water visible ahead.

Ben Johnson, the First Officer, is also a very experienced pilot having flown for the ill-fated Court Line before joining Britannia in 1973. Despite his years of flying, this is his first transatlantic flight as a pilot and he is pleased to be able to draw on Graham's vast store of experience. The rapidly growing popularity of the American holiday market, partly brought about by the introduction of economic twinjets such as the Boeing 767, has meant that many British pilots whose normal routine kept them flying on intra-European routes are now being introduced to the experience of long-range flying. Britannia Airways pilots are given a short course on EROPS techniques and then carry out a return long-range flight under the auspices of an ex-

break up and Newfoundland's rugged landscape is coming into view. This part of Canada is sparsely inhabited and apart from the occasional road and isolated settlement there is little sign of life. There are, of course, numerous lakes to be seen — a feature common to many areas of Canada.

ATC responsibility for the flight passes to Montreal Centre at 1805 with a frequency change to 133.35MHz and shortly afterwards the great St Lawrence River comes into view in the distance, sweeping in on the port side. The flightdeck is cleared of visitors as the cabin staff are about to serve the main meal of the flight to the passengers, It is also time for more refreshments on the flightdeck and again the two pilots are offered a choice of separately prepared hot dishes. The Captain elects to eat first this time, selecting an appetising curry dish, and is enjoying this as the aircraft turns over the Baie-Comeau VOR (code letters YBC) at 1834. The new track, 245°M, takes the flight directly along the path of the St Lawrence River.

Below:

The compact planar array of the Bendix radar is mounted in the nose of the 767. The loop aerials above and below are for the dual ILS localiser receivers.

perienced Captain before being considered qualified for these flights.

A few minutes after crossing Baie-Comeau, ATC passes instructions to contact the next Montreal sector on 135.02MHz. This time a woman's voice answers Ben's call. Most ATC authorities employ female controllers but Canadian legislation lays down that at least 10% of controllers should be female — a target which the Transportation Department has yet to reach. A reminder that we are now over the Canadian state of Quebec comes from listening to the controller at Montreal as she talks in French to several aircraft flying at lower levels in this section of airspace.

The flightdeck routine continues as the 767 cruises comfortably at 39,000ft. Despite the steady headwind, ground speed is around 420kt as the Charlevoix NDB is passed at 1849 and Quebec is reached at 1859 — almost exactly 6hr after take-off. Unfortunately a layer of cloud hides the interesting city, site of General Wolf's famous victory in 1759 during the Seven Years War. At this point the engines have consumed exactly 30 tonnes of fuel with just over 18 tonnes remaining. A check with the FMC display shows that there should be over seven

Above:
Dinner is served. The pilots take their meals on the flightdeck, but at different times and from different menus. On a long flight like this there will be two light meals as well as a steady supply of coffee or tea.

tonnes left, enough for almost 2hr flying on reaching Orlando. This is slightly up on the forecast total remaining (6,620kg) despite the longer routeing caused by the weather.

Passage over Quebec is the signal for another ATC frequency change, this time to 133.22. Routeing is on Jet 560 and the St Lawrence River is again in sight just below on the starboard side as the aircraft heads down towards the Plattsburgh VOR and United States airspace. Track is now 231°M and allowing for the magnetic variation, which is 18°W at this point, the true track is now 213°, approximately south-southwest — BAL326A is finally beginning to head south towards the sun!

After passing Montreal a constant electronic warbling noise becomes audible on the VHF radio — a possible transmission from an aircraft's Emergency Locator Beacon (ELB) on 121.5MHz. This is a device which is triggered automatically in the event of an aircraft accident and can be used by search and rescue aircraft

The CDU display as the 767 passes over Quebec (YQB) showing the next stages of the route. There are 57 miles to go to the FORJE intersection on a track of 232°. Speed is Mach 0.8 and altitude 39,000ft. PLB22 is a point 22 miles from Plattsburgh VOR and indicates the position of the US/Canadian border.

Below right:

This CDU display has been selected to the Progress mode and gives the pilots an up to date account of the flight. It shows that the Charlevoix NDB (ML) was crossed at 1850 and there are 61 miles to run to overhead Quebec which will be crossed at 1900. Fuel remaining, in tonnes, is shown in the righthand column. Looking ahead, it shows that Orlando (KMCO) will be reached at 2204 after flying a further 1,350 miles. The information at the lower edge of the screen shows which navigation aids are being used to provide positional data.

and ground parties to home in on the location. The transmission has obviously been heard and reported by other aircraft but the source has not yet been traced. The Montreal controller calls up to see in the Britannia pilots can add any information. Captain Freeman confirms that the transmissions are being picked up and also that the signal appears to be fading, presumably indicating that the source is some way behind us. Unfortunately the outcome of this little drama will remain a mystery as 2min later instructions for another frequency change are passed.

Montreal Control: 'Britannia Three One Six Alpha contact Boston One Three Five decimal Seven.'

After the long transatlantic haul and almost 800 miles over Canadian territory, Flight BAL316A is at last entering United States airspace. The time is 1925 and there are still over 1,200 miles to go but, somehow, Orlando suddenly seems much closer!

Switching to the new frequency, Ben makes contact and is rewarded with a clearance direct to Syracuse 150 miles ahead. At this time the aircraft is just reaching the Plattsburgh VOR situated adjacent to the huge USAF Air Base of the same name on the shores of Lake Champlain. The airfield stands out clearly and rows of parked B-52 bombers are just discernible on the acres of concrete ramp. While on the 20min run down to Syracuse the Captain takes the opportunity to update the passengers on the flight's progress and points out the vast expanse of Lake Ontario which is visible less than 50 miles away to starboard. During this time there are two

more frequency changes (Boston 123.87MHz and Cleveland Centre 133.95MHz) as the 767 cuts across the various ATC sectors. In fact for the next 30min control of the aircraft is passed from sector to sector every few minutes. The reason for this is that the southbound route is now beginning to cut across the multitude of east-west orientated airways radiating from the busy New York airports. Up to now there have been few, if any, other aircraft flying in close proximity but, after turning south at Syracuse, there are several sightings of crossing and opposite direction traffic. In each case the other aircraft is at least 2,000ft below in order to comply with ATC separation standards but, even so, a big aircraft such as a 747 looks very close at that distance. A KLM Boeing 747 passes in the opposite direction, shortly followed by a Continental DC-10 heading east towards New York.

Despite the increase in British charter flights to the United States, the sight of a Britannia Airways aircraft is still something of a rare event to most American pilots and the Continental captain is unable to restrain his curiosity as he passes below.

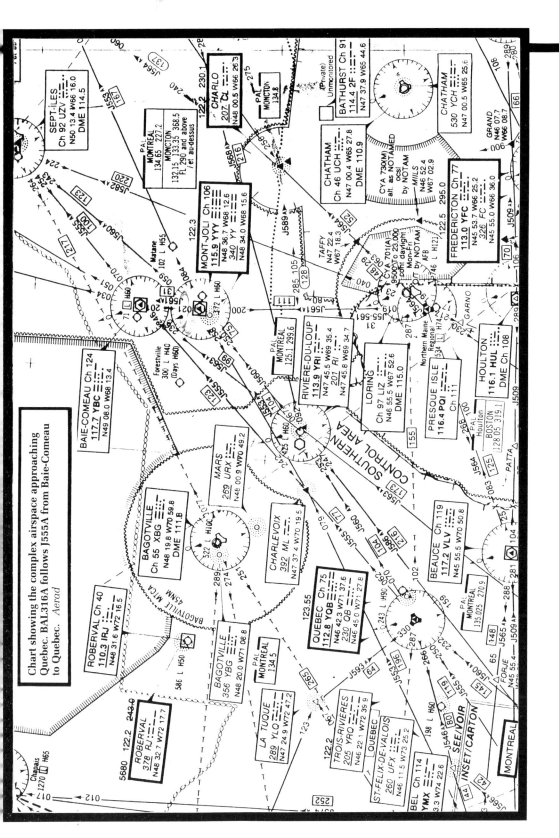

Chart showing the complex airspace approaching Quebec. BAL316A follows J555A from Baie-Comeau to Quebec. *Aerad*

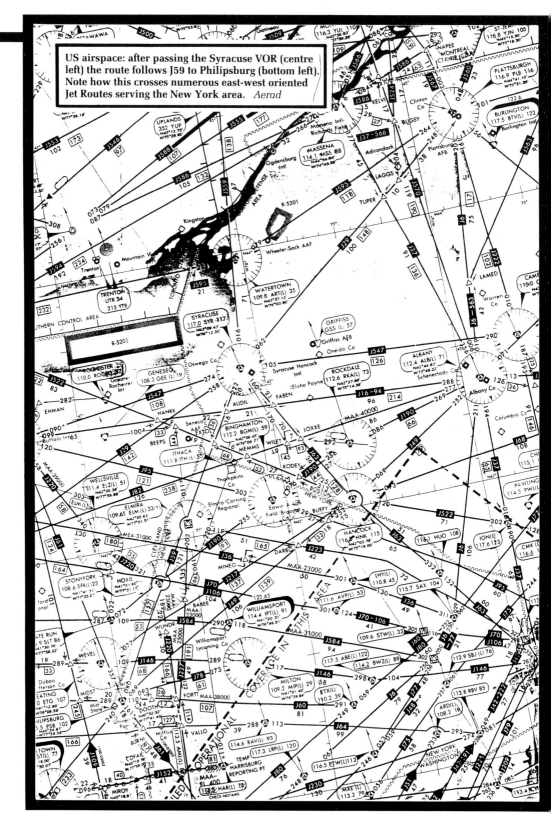

US airspace: after passing the Syracuse VOR (centre left) the route follows J59 to Philipsburg (bottom left). Note how this crosses numerous east-west oriented Jet Routes serving the New York area. *Aerad*

Continental Pilot: 'Er . . . New York, we just passed a Seven Six Seven with a lady painted on the tail . . . who is that?'

New York Centre: 'Continental Four Seven Eight . . . that's Britannia!'

Continental Pilot: 'Gee! Is that so. We thought it was Queen Boadicea!'

Graham Freeman smiles, but says nothing.

Having passed Syracuse at 1939, control of the aircraft has passed to New York Centre (ARCC) on 132.17 and in the next 100 miles control passes rapidly to three other New York sectors before being finally transferred again to Cleveland ARCC as BAL316A approaches Philipsburg VOR, 200 miles west of New York.

Unlike the European ATC system, American air traffic control is highly automated with all the ARCCs being linked to an advanced computerised data handling system. The FAA has been able to develop a nationwide system using standardised equipment and common procedures while the European network is made up of sovereign national ATC units often using non-compatible equipment. This means that the safe transfer of control between adjacent ATCCs sometimes entails time consuming telephone calls or the use of rigid and inefficient procedures which artificially restrict the flow of traffic.

In the FAA system all ARCCs are linked to a computerised network which stores details of all flights in American airspace and presents the relevant data on the controller's radar screen. As an aircraft approaches the boundary between adjacent sectors or ARCC areas of responsibility, the controller makes a few inputs to his keypad causing the aircraft symbol to be surrounded by a flashing ring. The computer notes this and causes a similar occurrence on the screen of the controller to whom the aircraft is being transferred, even though he may be in another ARCC hundreds of miles away. Details of the aircraft (identity, type, level, destination and route) are also displayed alongside the symbol. The receiving controller presses a key to indicate that he can accept the aircraft and the first controller instructs the aircraft to change frequency. Once the transfer has been effected, the second controller makes a further key input which cancels the flashing symbol on both screens. The whole procedure is accomplished in seconds without the need for any other communication between the controllers. On initial contact the controller advises 'Radar Contact' which signifies that the pilots are not required to make standard position reports and this cuts radio traffic to a minimum.

A side product of the sophisticated data handling capacity of the system is that information on all flights can be transmitted from coast to coast to a central point. Using this capability, the FAA has established a Flow Management Cell in Washington which monitors the flow of traffic on the various airways throughout the United States. Having this overall picture allows the instructions to be sent to the ARCCs on a tactical basis to re-route traffic in order to avoid bottlenecks and restrictions. This makes for a more efficient utilisation of airspace and allows the American ATC system to handle the explosive growth in airline traffic which has built up since commercial deregulation.

After Philipsburg, passed at 2001, the 767 settles on to a track of 240°M for the 173-mile leg to the Charleston VOR (ident code HVQ) on Jet 78. By now the flight is clearing the busy New York area and is integrating into the north-south routed system which serves the densely populated Eastern seaboard. At 2919 control is again

Left:
On a long flight the standard of the cabin service comes under close scrutiny. Britannia has an excellent reputation in this department and it is always service with a smile.

Above:
The seven-abreast seating on the 767 is very popular with passengers. The 2-4-2 configuration gives plenty of elbow room and the high cabin roof gives an air of spaciousness. Note the projector for the video system which is suspended from the roof and is visible in the top righthand corner of this photograph.

transferred, this time to the Indianapolis ARCC. The town of Charleston, up ahead, is the state capital of West Virginia and should not be confused with the better known port of Charleston which is in South Carolina. Today's flight has already passed over the States of New York, Pennsylvania and West Virginia and will cross parts of Virginia, North Carolina, South Carolina, Georgia and Florida before reaching Orlando. After crossing Charleston, the route turns almost due south and crosses over the Alleghany mountain range and then the famous Blue Ridge mountains. The dense and luxuriant growth of trees on the latter does indeed take on a blueish tinge when viewed from 39,000ft. However, the pilots have little time to take in the view. Orlando is now less than 90min flying time away and it is time to begin preparations for landing.

Above:
Bangor Airport in the State of Maine, on the American northeastern seaboard, is used for refuelling stops by some Britannia 767 flights from the UK. The length of runway at Prestwick has allowed today's flight BAL316A to uplift enough fuel for the whole journey and so this intermediate stop is not required.

Arrival

Orlando is one of the fastest growing airports in the United States, sharing in Florida's ever increasing popularity as a tourist centre and supporting a range of scheduled services to over 100 US cities. The number of passengers passing through has increased from just over one million in 1970 to over 17 million in 1990. Originally built as the McCoy Air Force Base, the airport authority took over the land surrounding the base when the USAF pulled out in 1974 and began construction of a new terminal complex in 1978, a process which continues today.

In order to cope with growth in traffic, new runways were laid down and today there are three in operation with a fourth under construction. These are grouped in two parallel pairs on a north-south orientation with the terminal complexes between them. The westerly pair are designated 18R/36L and 18L/36R (L/R=Left/Right). On the east side only 17/35 is operational. With a multiple runway set-up such as this the approach and landing procedures are likely to be complex and the crew of BAL316A now consult charts showing the Standard Arrival (STAR) and approach procedures.

As this is done, Charleston in now astern, crossed at 2033, and the aircraft is following a track of 186° on Jet 85 to the next waypoint, Spartanburg VOR, 154 miles ahead. From there it is approximately 400 miles to Orlando.

The charts show that, arriving from the north a LEESE STAR is the most likely and landing will probably be on either Runway 18L or 18R. While 18R is equipped with an ILS, the other has only a VOR DME procedure which gives no glidepath information and descent is based on distance from touchdown. The 18R ILS frequency is 111.9MHz and this is dialled up on the Captain's VOR/ILS selector ready for use. The selector is left in the AUTO mode leaving the FMS to continue selecting the VOR frequencies required for the continuing en route navigation.

Graham also takes the opportunity to run through the approach procedures with his First Officer and also briefs him on the action in the

Left:
Destination Orlando. A view of the airport showing the recently completed Runway 35/17 with its associated taxiways. Terminal and apron complexes are visible in the background. This busy airport will soon be handling over 20 million passengers a year. *Greater Orlando Aviation Authority*

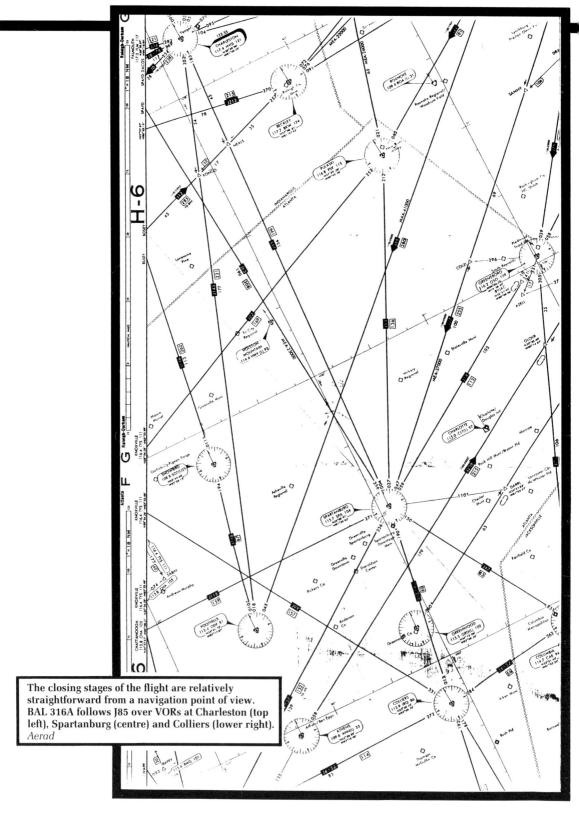

The closing stages of the flight are relatively
straightforward from a navigation point of view.
BAL 316A follows J85 over VORs at Charleston (top
left), Spartanburg (centre) and Colliers (lower right).
Aerad

event of having to break off the approach and go around. If this should be necessary, pressing the TO/GA (Take-Off/Go-Around) button on the Thrust Management System will immediately cause the autothrottle system to give full power for the climb-out.

Another transfer of control occurs at 2040 and the flight is now in contact with Atlanta Centre on 126.77MHz.

Atlanta Control: 'Britannia Three One Six Alpha Heavy radar contact. Maintain Three Nine Zero. Squawk Six Three Six One.'

This is the first change of transponder code since entering Canadian airspace three-and-a-half hours ago. The previous code, 0713, has provided identification to ATC as the 767 has been passed from one ATC unit to another, this information being stored in the computer network's database. The new code is one allocated to Orlando inbounds and is another sign that the flight is reaching its final stages.

Spartanburg is passed at 2104 and control transfers to another Atlanta frequency, 132.17MHz. In the meantime the pilots are checking the fuel state in order to calculate the aircraft's landing weight. 38,537kg of fuel have now been used after 8hrs flying and just under 10 tonnes remain. On this basis the landing weight should be 113 tonnes with over 8 tonnes of fuel remaining. Ben checks the 767 performance tables and reads off that the threshold landing speed (V Ref) is 130kt using 30° of flap. He enters these details on the blue landing card and places it on the centre console where it is easily visible. In addition he sets the bugs on the ASI to this figure and checks that the Captain's is correctly set.

While Ben has been occupied with this task and monitoring the ATC frequency which is becoming busier, the Captain selects frequency 121.25MHz on his VHF set in order to listen to the Orlando Automatic Terminal Information Service (ATIS). This is a continuously transmitted pre-recorded message giving out weather, runway and airfield data and is updated every 30min, each new message being given a code letter. The message contains a lot of information rattled off quickly in an unfamiliar American accent and it is often necessary to listen more than once in order to get everything noted down.

Orlando ATIS: 'This is Orlando Information Oscar. All departures call One Three Four Seven for clearance. On departure pass your callsign

and transponder code. Weather at two zero five two, four thousand five hundred scattered, visibility ten miles, wind two eight zero diagonal one nine, temperature nine zero dew point seven five, altimeter two nine nine seven. ILS approach Runway One Seven, visual approach Runway One Eight Left. Runway One Eight Right closed, taxiway five and nine closed, alpha to west ramp closed. All departures contact delivery on one three four seven with gate number and information oscar received.'

Amazingly Graham manages to get all this down in one go. The ATIS information is intended for both arriving and departing aircraft and prevents the other VHF channels becoming clogged with the repetitive passing of routine information. The weather is good for the landing and it appears that the heavy thunderstorm activity along the coast, and visible even from this distance, is not actually affecting the airfield. It is currently right in the middle of the Florida thunderstorm season which lasts through June, July and August, and these can present quite a hazard on occasions with the associated cumulo nimbus clouds sometimes rising as high as 55,000ft. A very heavy storm could cause the flight to be diverted to another airport but there are no such problems today.

After Spartanburg, the next fix is the Colliers VOR which is passed at 2112 and 5min later control is transferred to Jacksonville Centre on 135.97MHz. Ben makes the initial call.

First Officer: 'Jacksonville, Britannia Three One Six Alpha Heavy, Level Three Nine Zero.'

Jacksonville Control: 'Roger Three One Six Alpha, radar contact, cleared direct SWAMY for LEESE Six arrival Orlando.'

With the arrival procedure now confirmed, Ben is able to check through the routeing already entered in the FMS and also to enter the vertical profile required. The arrival procedure stipulates that point LEESE, 30 miles northwest of the Orlando VOR is to be crossed at 12,000ft and a speed of 250kts. By entering these parameters the pilot can ensure that, subject to ATC clearance, the autopilot will initiate descent at the appropriate point in order to achieve this. The point SWAMY is part of the LEESE procedure and is just over 130 mile north of Orlando. LEESE itself, although defined by a distance and radial from Orlando, actually coincides with the position of a small airport called Leesburg.

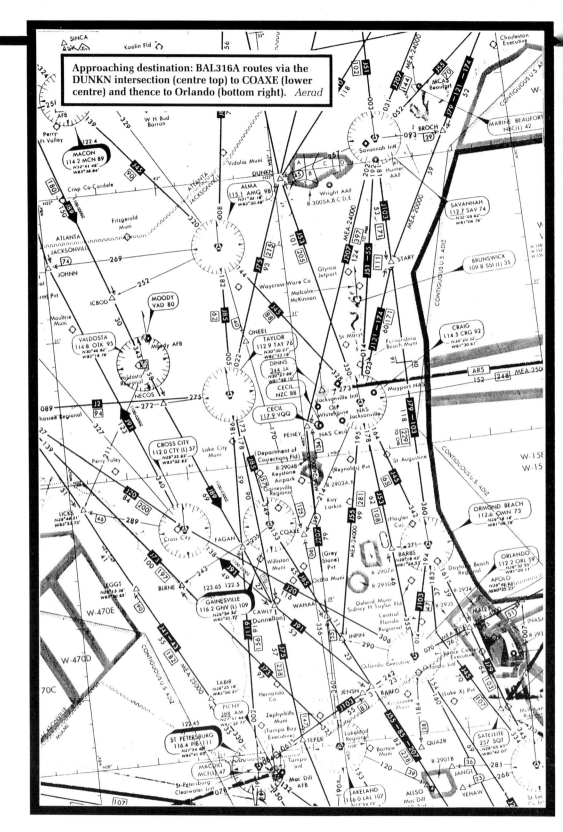

Approaching destination: BAL316A routes via the DUNKN intersection (centre top) to COAXE (lower centre) and thence to Orlando (bottom right). *Aerad*

Already the green symbol marking the point at which descent should begin is creeping down the EHSI screen, approximately 80 miles ahead. With the autopilot set in the VNAV mode the aircraft will maintain cruise power to the Top of Descent (TD) point and then reduce to minimum power, allowing the aircraft to descend steadily at around 1,500ft/min. Although this is the most efficient descent profile in terms of fuel economy, it has the disadvantage that a closure of the throttles after hours in the cruise results in a sudden and severe temperature drop for most of the engine components precipitating a condition known as Thermal Shock. While this is not normally dangerous in any way, repeated cycles could set up stress in vital components such as turbine blades. In order to prevent this and prolong engine life, the airline has developed a technique of starting descent slightly earlier than the calculated TD and only partially reducing engine power to give a flatter initial descent gradient. Subsequently power is further reduced as the nominal descent profile is intercepted and thereafter the aircraft is allowed to follow the VNAV profile.

With 50 miles to run to SWAMY, and 20 miles to TD, Ben calls ATC for descent clearance.

First Officer: 'Britannia Three One Six Alpha, request descent.'
Jacksonville Control: 'Roger Three One Six Alpha, cleared Flight Level Three One Zero.'

To initiate an early descent Ben sets 31,000ft in the Altitude Select box and uses the CDU keyboard, activating a DESCENT NOW prompt on the screen. This causes the autothrottle to reduce power (N1 at 80%) and, in order to maintain the preprogrammed cruise speed, the autopilot initiates pitch down into a descent. The caption VNAV SPD (Vertical Nav Speed) now appears on the pilot's EADI displays. Descent rate is just over 1,000ft/min and the aircraft will continue to descend in this mode until it intercepts the ideal descent profile as determined by the FMS. At this point the autothrottle will reduce to flight idle and descent rate will increase. As the FMS computer determines that the correct descent pattern has been set up, the EADI caption will change to VNAV PATH.

Meanwhile, in the main cabin the passengers will have become aware that power has been reduced and that the aircraft is descending. As he is likely to be very busy for the final part of the flight, Graham takes this last opportunity to speak to the passengers, informing them that

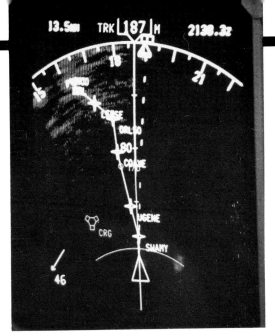

Above:
The EHSI display at 2138 shows the aircraft with 13.5nm to run to the SWAMY intersection. The route ahead runs through UGENE, COAXE, and LEESE to Orlando, which has just come on to the screen at top left. Note the wind vector in the lower left corner, indicating a headwind of 46kt.

Below:
The descent into Orlando has commenced. The altimeter shows that the aircraft is approaching 32,000ft and the VSI shows a descent rate of just under 1,500ft/min.

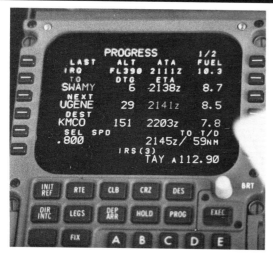

Left:
The CDU display shows 6 miles to go to SWAMY, ETA 2138, and 151 to Orlando. Arrival time is forecast as 2203 and there will be almost eight tonnes of fuel remaining.

descent into Orlando has commenced and that the aircraft should be on the ground within 30min. After passing on the weather conditions at the destination he ends on a cheerful note, expressing the hope that everybody will have a happy and successful holiday. This announcement is also noted by the cabin crew who now start their final rounds of collecting empty cups, glasses, trays and checking that seatback tables are stowed away. Once this is done another check is made that seat belts are correctly fastened before the Number One reports to the Captain that the cabin is secure for landing.

It is 2130 when descent is commenced, 8.5hrs after take-off. As the 767 drops through FL350, ATC calls again.

Jacksonville Control: 'Britannia Three One Six contact Jacksonville One Three Two decimal Eight Two.'

Ben switches over to the new frequency.

First Officer: 'Jacksonville Britannia Three One Six Alpha Heavy passing Three Five Zero.'
Jacksonville Control: 'Three One Six Alpha roger radar control. Maintain Three One Zero.'

This level is reached at 2133 and the aircraft levels off under the control of the autopilot exactly as it crosses the SWAMY fix – a tribute to the absolute precision of the computer-controlled autopilot.

First Officer: 'Britannia Three One Six Alpha level at Three One Zero passing SWAMY.'

Three minutes later, another call.

Jacksonville Control: 'Britannia Three One Six Alpha cleared Flight Level Two Seven Zero contact Jacksonville One Two Seven Five Five.'

As the Captain begins the descent, Ben checks with the new sector controller. More instructions are immediately forthcoming.

Jacksonville Control: 'Britannia Three One Six Alpha is cleared One Six Thousand on Two Nine Nine Seven. Expect to cross LEESE level at One Two Zero, speed Two Five Zero Knots.'

Graham now dials 16,000 in the altitude selector, checking that the altimeters are set to 29.97in so that they will read altitude correctly as the aircraft descends, now in VNAV PATH mode. Just after leaving FL310 another waypoint, UGENE, is passed – its passage confirmed by the purple symbol on the EHSI and a readout on the FMS display. A few minutes pass before another instruction comes from ATC.

Jacksonville Control: 'Britannia Three One Six Alpha descend to Twelve Thousand Feet, cross LEESE level.'

The Altitude Selector is again wound down to the newly cleared altitude and as the aircraft passes through 25,000ft on the descent the Captain calls for the Approach Checks. Ben picks up the checklist card and makes the calls.

First Officer: 'Briefing.'

The Captain quickly runs over the details of the approach.

Captain: 'We are making a LEESE Arrival and can expect radar vectoring to make an approach to Runway One Eight Left. Once we are visual I will disconnect the autopilot and make a manual approach and landing. In the event of a Go-Around give me full take-off power and we will climb to two thousand feet, turning left to intercept the One Six Two radial from the Orlando VOR. Safety altitude is two thousand eight hundred and our diversion airfield is Tampa, although as we have plenty of fuel in hand we can hold for at least an hour if required.'

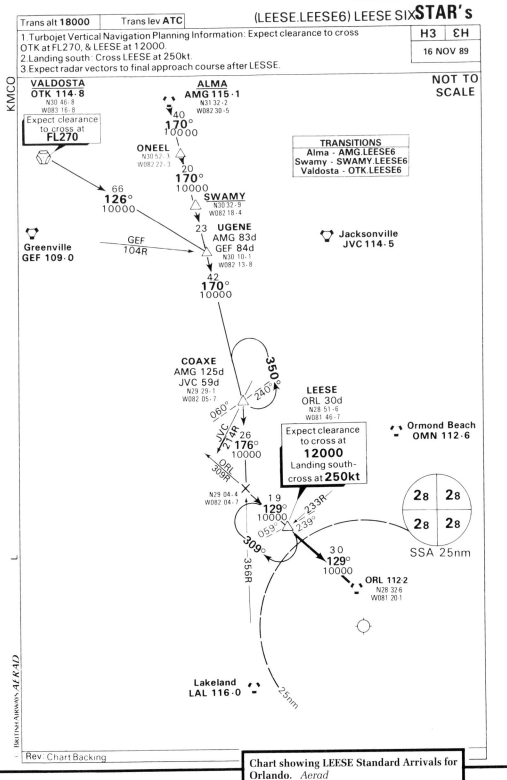

ORLANDO INTL
(LEESE.LEESE6) LEESE SIX STAR's

Chart showing LEESE Standard Arrivals for Orlando. *Aerad*

Trans alt **18000**	Trans lev **ATC**

1. Turbojet Vertical Navigation Planning Information: Expect clearance to cross OTK at FL270, & LEESE at 12000.
2. Landing south: Cross LEESE at 250kt.
3. Expect radar vectors to final approach course after LESSE.

H3	EH
16 NOV 89	

KMCO

NOT TO SCALE

VALDOSTA
OTK 114·8
N30 46·8
W083 16·8

Expect clearance to cross at **FL270**

ALMA
AMG 115·1
N31 32·2
W082 30·5

40
170°
10000

ONEEL
N30 52·3
W082 22·3
20
170°
10000

66
126°
10000

SWAMY
N30 32·9
W082 18·4

23 **UGENE**
AMG 83d
GEF 84d
N30 10·1
W082 13·8

GEF
104R

Greenville
GEF 109·0

42
170°
10000

TRANSITIONS
Alma - AMG.LEESE6
Swamy - SWAMY.LEESE6
Valdosta - OTK.LEESE6

Jacksonville
JVC 114·5

COAXE
AMG 125d
JVC 59d
N29 29·1
W082 05·7

350°
240°
060°
JVC
214R
26
176°
10000
ORL
309R

LEESE
ORL 30d
N28 51·6
W081 46·7

Expect clearance to cross at **12000** Landing south- cross at **250kt**

Ormond Beach
OMN 112·6

N29 04·4
W082 04·7

19
129°
10000
059° 233R
239°

309°
356R

28	28
28	28

SSA 25nm

30
129°
10000

ORL 112·2
N28 32·6
W081 20·1

Lakeland
LAL 116·0

25nm

BRITISH AIRWAYS *AERAD*

Rev: Chart Backing

listening out for a gap in the almost continuous stream of instructions to other inbound aircraft Ben is able to make his contact call. The controller replies immediately.

Orlando Radar: 'Britannia Three One Six descend to Seven Thousand Feet.'

This instruction comes just in time to save levelling off as BA316A crosses the LEESE intersection at exactly 12,000ft with speed steadying at 250kts. Still in conformity with the STAR, the autopilot turns the aircraft left on to a heading of 132° and Graham closes the speedbrakes now that the speed has stabilised. On the 767 the speedbrakes consist of seven movable surfaces on the upper side of each wing's trailing edge. These are raised in proportion to the degree of movement of the control lever, allowing a very precise degree of control. 7,000ft is now set on the altitude selector.

A few minutes after passing LEESE, ATC starts to steer the aircraft into the final approach sequence.

Orlando Radar: 'Britannia Three One Six turn left heading One One Zero.'

Ben acknowledges this and continues to the next check.

First Officer: 'Autobrakes.'
Captain: 'Set'.

He reaches down to confirm that the wheelbrake control is set to '2' which will give a moderate deceleration after landing.

First Officer: 'Airspeed Bugs.'
Captain: 'Set.'
First Officer: 'Altimeters.'
Captain: 'QNH Two Nine Nine Seven set and cross-checked.'
First Officer: 'Approach aids.'
Captain: 'Checked and set.'
First Officer: 'Recall.'
Captain: 'Checked and clear.'
First Officer: 'Approach checks complete.'

The aircraft is now descending steadily at 1,500ft/min and airspeed is 280kt. Graham dials up 250kts on the autopilot speed selector and reaches down to the speedbrake lever set in the centre console to the left of the thrust levers.

While the First Officer continues to monitor the ATC frequency, the Captain now contacts the Delta Airlines Operations Centre at Orlando on its company frequency to pass on the ETA for landing and gives details of the passenger load. Delta is responsible for the ground handling of Britannia aircraft and the centre acknowledges the call advising that the aircraft will be parked on Gate 24 on Airside 1 Ramp.

With 13 miles to run to LEESE, ATC call up with instructions to contact Orlando Radar on 120.15MHz. This is duly carried out and after

Below:
The speed brake lever is conveniently to hand alongside the throttle quadrant. Use of the brakes allows very precise speed control when manoeuvring in the final stages of a flight.

VFR Chart showing the Orlando area. Note the NASA base at Cape Canaveral on the coast to the east.

This is acknowledged and the Captain dials up the heading on the autopilot before deselecting LNAV and pressing the Heading Hold button. Under ATC vectoring the aircraft's route will vary from that entered in the FMS as the nominal approach route, so that the LNAV facility is now redundant. In addition Graham switches from VNAV to FL CH (Flight Level Change) mode which is more suited to the constant descent clearances which are part of the approach routines to any busy airport.

The time is now 2156 and there are less than 20 miles left to run to touchdown. As the aircraft descends to the lower altitudes the flat Florida landscape takes on more detail and, approaching the airport from the northwest, several large lakes are visible and the sprawling mass of skyscrapers which is the city of Orlando lies just ahead.

Orlando Radar: 'Britannia Three One Six contact Approach One Two Seven Seven Five.'

Another frequency change.

First Officer: 'Orlando Approach, Britannia Three One Six Heavy level at Seven Zero steering One One Zero.'
Orlando Approach: 'Roger Three One Six, maintain Seven Thousand. Vectoring for visual approach One Eight Left. Report field in sight.'

Thirty seconds later further descent is given.

Orlando Approach: 'Britannia Three One Six descend to Four Thousand Feet. Contact Orlando One Two Four Eight.'

Despite the number of aircraft movements at the airport, the ATC system is superficially very simple. The two sets of runways are treated virtually as separate airfields and traffic inbound from the west and northwest is directed through LEESE for Runway 18 L/R while traffic from the east and northeast is directed through another point, BITHO, for the Runway 17, Inbound traffic crosses both points at 12,000ft and thereafter is vectored to the final approach path through blocks of airspace which have progressively lower vertical dimensions by three consecutive teams of controllers, each responsible for a particular block of airspace. Departing flights are allocated to the east or west runway complexes, depending on the direction of their routeing after take-off. Standard departure routes (SIDs) are laid down which neatly weave above or below the inbound airspace blocks so that the

departure controllers then have their own discrete sections of airspace in which to climb the outbound aircraft. This system explains the number of radio frequency changes while on approach to the airport.

Still in HDG SEL and FL CH autopilot modes, the Captain dials up 4,000ft in compliance with the last instruction and causes descent from 7,000ft to begin, although speed remains at 250kt, as set on the speed indicator.

In the meantime the First Officer has contacted the next ATC frequency and receives further instructions.

Orlando Radar: 'Britannia Three One Six cleared right turn direct Orlando VOR, descend to Three Thousand Feet.'

This is acknowledged and Graham uses the heading selector to come round on to a heading of 150°, at the same time dialling up a speed of 190kt in order to slow down for the final approach. The airfield is less than 20 miles ahead but not yet visible as the 767 drops through patches of cloud.

Captain: 'Autopilot Disengage.'

Ben reaches up and presses the white strip at the lower righthand edge of the autopilot selector panel, allowing the Captain to take control of the aircraft manually. The AFCS is now disconnected and Graham reaches down to the throttle quadrants to deselect the autothrottle system. This is done by twice pressing a button inset into the handle at the top of each thrust lever. Two presses are necessary in order to cancel the aural warning which normally sounds when the autothrottle is disengaged.

With the throttles held back in the flight idle position, Graham again applies some speedbrake to assist in slowing the aircraft. In the meantime, Ben winds 135kt on to the speed selector and the red bug on both the ASIs move to this position. This speed is V Ref plus 5kt and will be the target speed on short final.

Approaching 3,000ft the aircraft is below cloud and the airfield now comes into sight, materialising slowly from the distant haze to the right of the nose. Ben advises ATC.

First Officer: 'Britannia Three One Six has the field in sight.'
Orlando Radar: 'Roger Three One Six, descend to Two Thousand Five Hundred, maintain until passing the VOR, cleared visual approach Runway One Eight Left.'

Above:
A wide-angle view of Orlando from the flightdeck. Runways 18L and 18R are visible ahead on the co-pilot's side, while the central area and other runway complexes can be seen away to the left.

As speed drops through 210kt Graham calls for the flaps to be lowered.

Captain: 'Flaps five.'

Ben moves the flap control lever back to the 5° mark and both pilots check the indicator in the centre of the instrument panel as they deploy. Operation of the flap lever also deploys the leading edge flaps to be opened in synchronisation with the trailing edge flaps. A setting of 1° is available which causes the flaps to slide rearwards increasing lift without appreciable corresponding increase in drag. Subsequent selections of 5°, up to a maximum of 30°, deflects the flaps increasingly downwards and causes full extension of the leading edge surfaces.

Although the airfield is now in sight, the multiple runway layout makes it essential that the correct runway is identified before turning on to final approach. Graham therefore continues heading towards VOR until both pilots are confident that they have the assigned runway identified. In the meantime the flightdeck door opens as the Number One looks in to report 'Cabin secure for landing' and places the confirmatory tag in its slot.

Captain: 'Undercarriage down.'

The limiting speed for lowering the undercarriage is 270kt and the 767 is well within that as Ben pushes the lever to the DOWN position. The clutch of indicators above the lever light up, two ambers showing that the doors and gear are unlocked, and then extinguishing in favour of three green showing NOSE, LEFT, RIGHT.

Orlando Radar: 'Britannia Three One Six contact Tower One Two Four Two.'

Ben checks in with the tower.

Orlando Tower: 'Britannia Three One Six, cleared to land One Eight Left, wind Two Seven Zero at One Five.'

The runway is eight miles ahead now and as the aircraft passes 3,000ft the Captain calls for the Landing Checks.

Below:
Five miles out. The Captain is now flying the aircraft manually. Altitude is 2,340ft and airspeed 155kt. The First Officer is dialling up 2,000ft on the altitude selector as this will be the required altitude in the event of a missed approach.

71

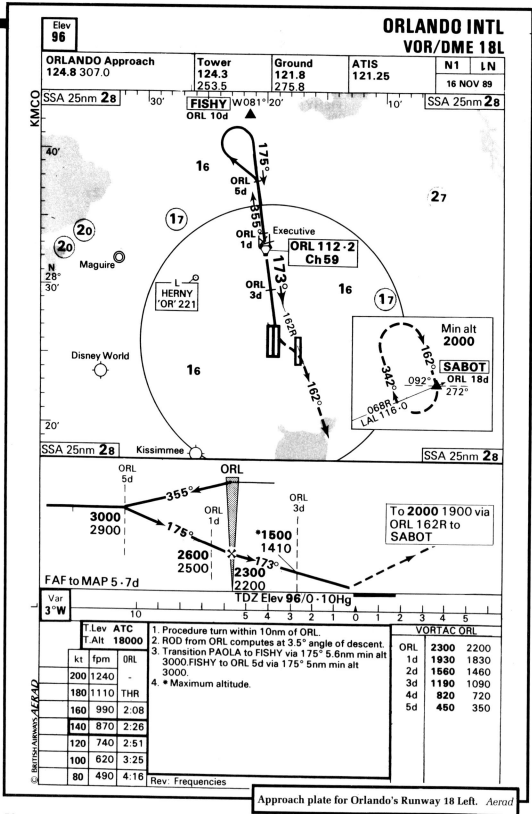

ORLANDO INTL
VOR/DME 18L

| Elev **96** | ORLANDO Approach **124.8** 307.0 | Tower **124.3** 253.5 | Ground **121.8** 275.8 | ATIS **121.25** | N1 LN **16 NOV 89** |

Approach plate for Orlando's Runway 18 Left. *Aerad*

Left:
The autobrake control is at the base of the instrument panel and can be set to give a preset deceleration after landing.

First Officer: 'Speedbrakes.'
Captain: 'Armed.'

This ensures that as soon as the wheels touch the ground the speedbrakes will automatically deploy, killing lift over the wing and helping to slow the aircraft down.

First Officer: 'Landing gear.'
Captain: 'Down.'
First Officer: 'Flaps.'
Captain: 'Flaps thirty.'

Ben moves the flap lever fully back, checks the indicator and calls 'Flaps thirty'. With the flaps fully extended, speed drops further to 160kt as the 767 crosses the Orlando VOR at 2,500ft.

The VOR is actually sited on another airport, Orlando Executive, situated only five miles from the international airport and right on the approach to the latter's runways. The Executive airport was originally Orlando's main civil airport until the USAF handed over the McCoy

AFB for development, although there are still over 400 general aviation aircraft based on this busy airfield. However, these are only permitted to fly up to 1,500ft in the airfield vicinity and this is the reason why inbound aircraft to the international airport are instructed to maintain 2,500ft until crossing the VOR. The situation is rather like having the busy Biggin Hill airfield situated under Heathrow's final approach — a set-up which would probably not be tolerated in the United Kingdom, but which is common in the US with its much greater general aviation activity.

Once past the VOR, Graham is free to concentrate on the final approach and landing. Turning right to line up with the runway, he reduces the power and begins to descend. A slight touch of speedbrake brings the speed back to 145kt. Three miles from touchdown a loud mechanical voice suddenly annunciates 'GLIDESLOPE, GLIDESLOPE'. This is the Ground Proximity Warning System which automatically triggers warnings if the aircraft's trajectory moves outside the parameters required for safe terrain clearance. The glideslope warning is normally a cautionary signal that the aircraft is going below the nominal 3° approach slope to the runway. On this occasion the warning has been triggered because the ILS has been set up for an approach to Runway 18R, although the aircraft is actually making a visual apprach to 18L which is not ILS equipped, and can be safely disregarded. The Captain applies a little extra power to stabilise the descent rate. However, he is now concentrating on the lights of the Visual Approach Slope Indicators visible to the left of the runway landing threshold. A combination of red and white lights allow him to maintain the correct rate of descent without taking his eyes off the runway.

First Officer: 'Five hundred feet.'

This is a standard warning call and the aircraft is now less than two miles from touchdown. Ben continues to call out speeds, allowing the Cap-

Left:
A touch of power on short final. The aircraft is passing through 300ft and airspeed is right on Vref, 135kt.

Left:
Two miles from touchdown. Note the confusing
number of runways and taxiways which can be seen.
Pilots must be extremely careful to ensure that they
have correctly identified their assigned runway.

Centre left:
One mile! Details of the airfield are clearly visible
now. There is an aircraft waiting for take-off and the
lights of the VASI system can be seen to the left of the
runway. These indicate to the pilot whether he is on
the correct glideslope.

Bottom left:
Over the threshold. The last seconds of any flight are
always the most crucial as the pilot works to achieve
a smooth touchdown.

tain to concentrate on the final stages of the
landing.

First Officer: 'One forty . . . One forty . . . Two
hundred feet . . . One three five . . . steady one
three five . . .'

The big 767 sweeps over the traffic-filled free-
way at the airfield boundary as Graham eases
back on the power, momentarily checks descent
rate with a rearward pressure on the control column, and flares gracefully on to the runway.
The time is 2203 — 9hr and 3min from take-off
at Prestwick.

Captain: 'Speedbrakes . . . Ground Idle.'

Ben checks that the speedbrakes have deployed
and moves the thrust levers right back against
the Ground Idle stop. Already speed is falling
below 110kt as the Captain selects '3' on the
autobrakes, increasing retardation. In addition,
he calls for reverse thrust and Ben obliges by
pulling up and back the top section of the thrust
levers.

Orlando Tower: 'Three One Six clear first available left, contact Ground One Two One Eight.'

Already another aircraft is lining up behind for
take-off. As speed drops further, to below 80kt,
Graham transfers steering control from the rudder pedals to the hand tiller and looks ahead for
a suitable turn-off from the runway. At the same
time he calls for reverse thrust to be cancelled
and the engine noise level drops right back as
this is done. A pair of taxiways loom up on the
left and with speed down to less than 40kt he
takes the second and moves clear of the runway.

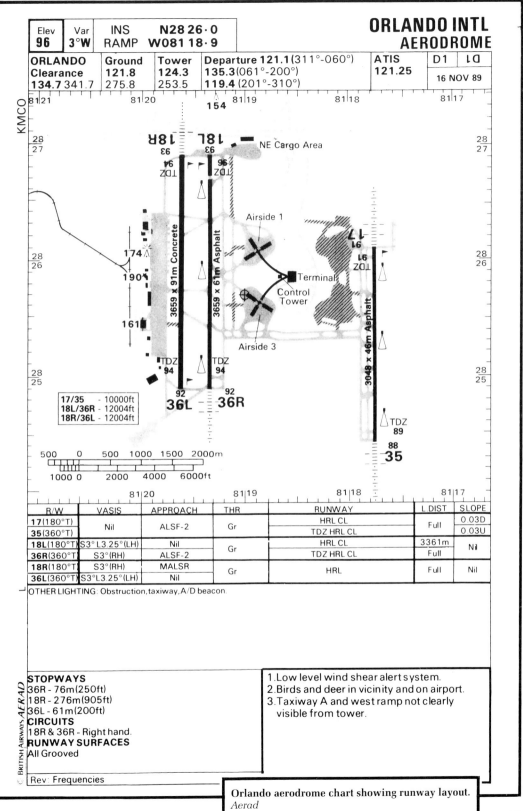

Elev 96	Var 3°W	INS RAMP	N28 26·0 W081 18·9				
ORLANDO Clearance 134.7 341.7	**Ground 121.8** 275.8	**Tower 124.3** 253.5	**Departure 121.1**(311°-060°) **135.3**(061°-200°) **119.4** (201°-310°)		**ATIS 121.25**	**D1**	**D1**

16 NOV 89

KMCO

NE Cargo Area

Airside 1

Terminal

Control Tower

Airside 3

TDZ

17/35   - 10000ft
18L/36R - 12004ft
18R/36L - 12004ft

36L   36R

35

500 0 500 1000 1500 2000m
1000 0   2000   4000   6000ft

R/W	VASIS	APPROACH	THR	RUNWAY		L.DIST	SLOPE
17(180°T)	Nil	ALSF-2	Gr	HRL CL		Full	0.03D
35(360°T)				TDZ HRL CL			0.03U
18L(180°T)	S3°L3.25°(LH)	Nil	Gr	HRL CL		3361m	Nil
36R(360°T)	S3°(RH)	ALSF-2		TDZ HRL CL		Full	
18R(180°T)	S3°(RH)	MALSR	Gr	HRL		Full	Nil
36L(360°T)	S3°L3.25°(LH)	Nil					

OTHER LIGHTING: Obstruction, taxiway, A/D beacon.

STOPWAYS
36R - 76m (250ft)
18R - 276m (905ft)
36L - 61m (200ft)
CIRCUITS
18R & 36R - Right hand.
RUNWAY SURFACES
All Grooved

1. Low level wind shear alert system.
2. Birds and deer in vicinity and on airport.
3. Taxiway A and west ramp not clearly visible from tower.

Rev: Frequencies

Orlando aerodrome chart showing runway layout.
Aerad

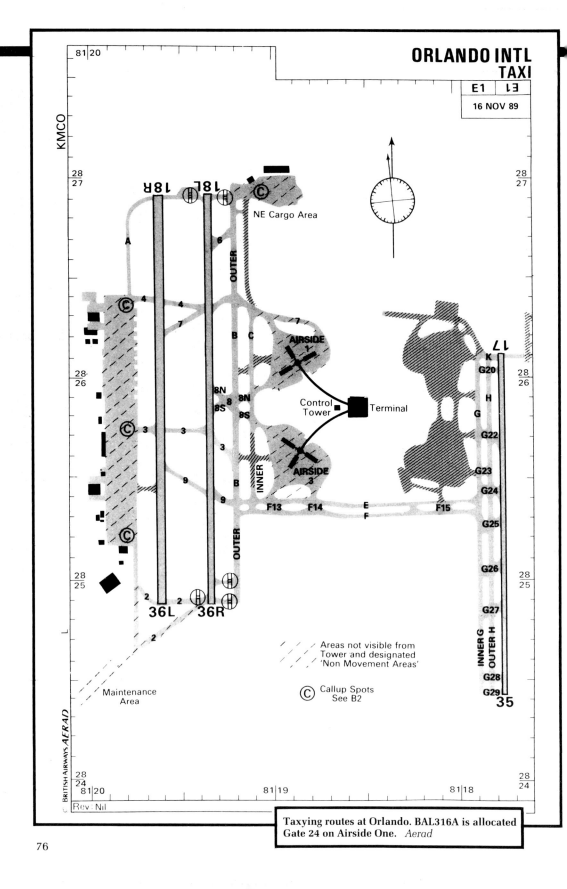

KMCO

81 20

28 27

18R   18L

NE Cargo Area

A

6

OUTER

C

4   4

7

B   C

7

AIRSIDE
1

Control
Tower

Terminal

28 26

8N
8S

8   8N
    8S

3   3

3

B

INNER

AIRSIDE
3

9

9

F13   F14   E   F   F15

28 25

2   2

OUTER

36L   36R

2

L

28 24

81 20   81 19   81 18

K

17

G20

28 26

H

G

G22

G23

G24

G25

G26

28 25

G27

INNER G   OUTER H

G28

G29

35

Areas not visible from
Tower and designated
'Non Movement Areas'

C   Callup Spots
See B2

Maintenance
Area

BRITISH AIRWAYS AERAD

Rev: Nil

Taxying routes at Orlando. BAL316A is allocated
Gate 24 on Airside One.   Aerad

76

Above:
Taxying in, leading and trailing edge flaps have been retracted.

Captain: 'Speedbrakes in . . . Autobraking disarmed . . . Flaps up.'

The First Officer quickly checks these items and raises the flaps before calling up on the ground frequency.

First Officer: 'Orlando Ground, Britannia Three One Six Alpha has vacated the runway, taxiing for Gate Twenty Four.'

The ground controller acknowledges as the pilots now check the aerodrome chart to establish the location of Gate 24. Recent developments at Orlando have created a system of satellite terminals each connected to the main terminal by modern Rapid Transit Systems, similar to that used to connect the North and South Terminals at Gatwick. Orlando's terminals are all situated between the runway pairs and each satellite has three radiating piers accommodating 24 boarding gates. The two western terminals, Airside One and Two, have been open for a few years and the new Airside Four was opened in 1990. Most of the British tour operators use Airside 1, the northerly of the two western terminals.

After coming off Runway 18L, the Britannia 767 swings left again to follow the outer parallel taxiway past Airside 2 before turning right and heading towards the acres of concrete ramp surrounding Airside 1. Orlando must be one of the most attractive airports in the world with each terminal and its taxiways surrounded by landscaped grounds including large lakes bordered by tropical vegetation — lakes which are known to contain several alligators! Looking out from the aircraft, the passengers certainly get a sense of having arrived somewhere different and exciting.

Gate 24 is on the northeasterly pier of the terminal, entailing several minutes taxiing at a steady pace, and as Graham steers around the last corner, another Britannia 767 is visible parked at Gate 27. Following the yellow guidelines, Graham slows the aircraft down to a walking pace as he swings in towards the gate and picks up a ground marshaller to wave him in. Cautiously edging forward, he stops as the marshaller gives the crossed arm signal. The parking brake is set and operation of the fuel cut-off

Below:
Despite all the modern technology involved in today's flying, there is almost always a marshaller giving the traditional hand signals to guide the pilot over the last few yards to his parking spot.

switches causes the engines to spool down as the pilots run through the shutdown checks.

First Officer: 'Hydraulics.'
Captain: 'Set.'
First Officer: 'Fuel System.'
Captain: 'Off.'
First Officer: 'Flaps.'
Captain: 'Up.'
First Officer: 'Speedbrakes.'
Captain: 'Down.'
First Officer: 'Parking Brake.'
Captain: 'Set.'
First Officer: 'Fuel Control.'
Captain: 'Cut-off.'

Finally, pressing a few keys on the AIDS panel produces a printout of essential data relating to the flight including take-off and landing times, time en route, maximum altitude, fuel burn and various engine parameters. This is attached to the aircraft's technical log for use by base engineers when drawing up and monitoring the aircraft's technical history.

By now the cabin crew have opened the aircraft's doors and the ground crew have positioned the walkways which connect to the terminal gate so that the passengers can begin disembarking. The pilots complete their paperwork, file away the various charts and clear away the rubbish which has accumulated in the course of the 9hr flight. A Delta Airlines engineer comes on to the flightdeck, ready to start his check of the aircraft for its return flight and the Captain is able to report that there have been no

Above:
Homeward Bound. Another Britannia crew about to leave their hotel in Orlando for the airport and to fly India Golf back to the UK.

technical problems or unserviceabilities on the flight from Scotland.

Once the passengers have disembarked, the pilots and cabin crew collect their own baggage from a compartment behind the flightdeck and make their way into the terminal, leaving India Golf ready for the next crew. Once through the immigration procedures, a minibus will be ready to take them off to their hotel. Unfortunately, the calls of the airline mean that they will only have a 24hr stopover in Orlando before picking up a UK-bound flight the following day. On another occasion they might be more fortunate and have two or three days rest, allowing time for a little sightseeing.

To the crew, the flight they have just made may seem a routine operation — as indeed it was. But it is easy to forget the organisation, training, experience and technical advances which have made such flights an everyday and completely safe event. Hopefully this book has given an insight into these matters, but the reader should remember that this was not a one-off flight, but one of hundreds flown by the airline with its Boeing 767s every year without incident — a testimony to the dedication and professionalism of all concerned.